POETRY
OF THE
CIVIL WAR

Edited by John Boyes

GRAMERCY BOOKS

NEW YORK

Published by Gramercy Books, an imprint of Random House Value Publishing, a division of Random House, Inc., New York, by arrangement with Arcturus Publishing Limited.

Gramercy is a registered trademark and the colophon is a trademark of Random House, Inc.

Random House
New York • Toronto • London • Sydney • Auckland
www.randomhouse.com

Printed and bound in China

Editor: Belinda Jones
Designer: Zoe Mellors

A catalog record for this title is available from the Library of Congress.

ISBN-13: 978-0-517-22877-7
ISBN-10: 0-517-22877-7

10 9 8 7 6 5 4 3 2 1

CONTENTS

INTRODUCTION

On January 17, 1861, mere weeks after South Carolina became the first state to formally secede from the Union, there appeared in *The Boston Evening Transcript* a poem entitled 'A Word for the Hour'. It was a remarkable piece of verse invoking images of fratricide, suicide and the Apocalypse. The author, the Quaker poet John Greenleaf Whittier, had long prophesied and dreaded a conflict. He counseled against war, arguing that the Union should continue, lesser in number, but on a higher moral plain. Though he would have preferred otherwise, the poem became the first significant piece of verse inspired by what is commonly called the American Civil War.

Other poems followed, two of the earliest being, 'Brother Jonathan's Lament for Sister Caroline' (page 12) by Oliver Wendell Holmes Sr, and 'Over the River' (page 96) by Jane T. H. Cross. Both predate the fighting and are apt reflections of the uncertainty of the time. Northerner Holmes instructs 'rash sister' Caroline (South Carolina) not to forget 'the pathway that leads to our door', while Southerner Cross writes of separating 'as friends of years should part,/With pleasant words and wishes'. From our vantage point, fourteen decades in the future, both poems seem naïve, almost fatuous; indeed they appeared so, shortly after their respective publications, as it was not long before fighting broke out and hatred and hostility found voice in the poetry of the Union and the Confederacy.

In 'Farewell to Brother Jonathan' (page 98), written in response to 'Brother Jonathan's Lament for Sister Caroline', the poet 'Caroline' rejects the advice of her 'cold-hearted brother, with tyrannous hand', turning away from the 'pathway that leads to the Pharisee's door...To the path through the valley and shadow of death!'

Holmes was changed by the war. In 'To Canaän!' (page 25) we find that the 'hasty', 'child of the sun' South Carolina of his earlier poem, has with its Confederate sisters, become 'rebel' and 'heathen'. 'The Lord has led us forth,' he writes, 'To strike upon the captive's chain/The hammers of the North.' Many of the Union poets, Holmes, Henry Wadsworth Longfellow, and Julia Ward Howe among them, were vocal abolitionists. For these poets, the war was not so much about the preservation of the Union, as put forth by Abraham Lincoln, as it was an exalted fight to defeat slavery. In fact, Whittier's last great poem of the war 'Laus Deo!' (page 73), beginning 'It is done!/Clang of bell and roar of gun', has naught to do with the end of fighting; rather it is a celebration of Lincoln's approval of the resolution proposing the Thirteenth Amendment.

Many of the more accomplished poems, particularly those of the South, have as their subjects individuals. Eulogies to generals Albert Sidney Johnston, Turner Ashby ('Black Knight of the Confederacy'), Stonewall Jackson, John Pegram, and Patrick Cleburne, serve as a reminder of the heavy losses in military leadership suffered by the Confederate States. Yet, it is interesting to note that two of the more memorable poems concern soldiers who would have otherwise been lost to history.

Isaac Newton Giffen (c.1848–1865), 'Little Giffen' of Francis Orray Ticknor's poem (page 167), was a young Confederate soldier who had been cared for by the poet, a medical doctor, and his wife. Give up for dead, the couple nursed Giffen back to health, and taught him to read and write. He was killed during one of the closing battles of the war, just months after leaving the Ticknor home.

'Your Letter, Lady, Came Too Late' (page 160), was composed by W. S. Hawkins whilst a prisoner at Camp Chase in Ohio, and is said to have been inspired by the story of a fellow imprisoned soldier named DeMoville.

Looking over the poetry inspired by the Civil War, one can't help but notice many great names of American literature: Walt Whitman, Emily Dickinson, Herman Melville, Ralph Waldo Emerson, Holmes, Longfellow, and the once-celebrated, now sadly neglected Whittier; and yet the most significant verse of the era was not by any of these. Though not the best poem to come out of the war, Francis Miles Finch's 'The Blue and The Gray' (page 91) had an impact which, without argument, continues to this day.

The origins of Finch's poem can be traced back to April 25, 1866, when, at Friendship Cemetery in Columbus, Mississippi, four Southern women met to decorate the graves of Confederate and Union soldiers. This act of generosity and reconciliation was widely reported by the nation's press, particularly in *The New York Tribune*, through which Finch found his inspiration. Following publication in the September 1867 issue of *The Atlantic Monthly*, 'The Blue and The Gray' achieved great popularity. The poem was immediately set to music, and contributed greatly to the effort to create a special day, Memorial Day, upon which to decorate Union and Confederate graves.

The movement was not without its detractors – witness 'To E.S. Salomon' (page 85), Ambrose Bierce's effective reproach of a California National Guardsman who fought against the decoration of Confederate war graves – but the ready adoption of this tradition serves to indicate the strength of the desire for reconciliation. Thus, we have Northerner Julia Ward Howe, author of the great Union anthem 'The Battle Hymn of the Republic', penning 'Robert E. Lee' (page 89), upon the Southern general's death. Here Lee is remembered as a 'gallant foeman in the fight/A brother when the fight was o'er'.

The latest poem in this collection belongs to Ambrose Bierce, a Union officer. Written some four decades after Whittier's 'A Word for the Hour' (page 10), 'A Year's "Casualties"' (page 90) alludes to Stonewall Jackson's dying words in lamenting the toll of the passage of time upon Civil War veterans. It was an exaction that continued well into the twentieth century, ending with the death of Albert H. Woolson, the last Civil War veteran on August 2, 1956.

THE BLUE

A Word for the Hour

The firmament breaks up. In black eclipse
Light after light goes out. One evil star,
Luridly glaring through the smoke of war,
As in the dream of the Apocalypse,
Drags others down. Let us not weakly weep
Nor rashly threaten. Give us grace to keep
Our faith and patience; wherefore should we leap
On one hand into fratricidal fight,
Or, on the other, yield eternal right,
Frame lies of law, and good and ill confound?
What fear we? Safe on freedom's vantage-ground
Our feet are planted: let us there remain
In unrevengeful calm, no means untried
Which truth can sanction, no just claim denied,
The sad spectators of a suicide!

They break the links of Union: shall we light

The fires of hell to weld anew the chain

On that red anvil where each blow is pain?

Draw we not even now a freer breath,

As from our shoulders falls a load of death

Loathsome as that the Tuscan's victim bore

When keen with life to a dead horror bound?

Why take we up the accursed thing again?

Pity, forgive, but urge them back no more

Who, drunk with passion, flaunt disunion's rag

With its vile reptile-blazon. Let us press

The golden cluster on our brave old flag

In closer union, and, if numbering less,

Brighter shall shine the stars which still remain.

JOHN GREENLEAF WHITTIER

Brother Jonathan's Lament
for Sister Caroline

(March 25, 1861)

She has gone, – she has left us in passion and pride, –
Our stormy-browed sister, so long at our side!
She has torn her own star from our firmament's glow,
And turned on her brother the face of a foe!

Oh, Caroline, Caroline, child of the sun,
We can never forget that our hearts have been one, –
Our foreheads both sprinkled in Liberty's name,
From the fountain of blood with the finger of flame!

You were always too ready to fire at a touch;
But we said, "She is hasty, – she does not mean much."
We have scowled, when you uttered some turbulent threat;
But Friendship still whispered, "Forgive and forget!"

Has our love all died out? Have its altars grown cold?
Has the curse come at last which the fathers foretold?
Then Nature must teach us the strength of the chain
That her petulant children would sever in vain.

They may fight till the buzzards are gorged with their spoil,
Till the harvest grows black as it rots in the soil,
Till the wolves and the catamounts troop from their caves,
And the shark tracks the pirate, the lord of the waves:

In vain is the strife! When its fury is past,
Their fortunes must flow in one channel at last,
As the torrents that rush from the mountains of snow
Roll mingled in peace through the valleys below.

Our Union is river, lake, ocean, and sky:

Man breaks not the medal, when God cuts the die!

Though darkened with sulphur, though cloven with steel,

The blue arch will brighten, the waters will heal!

Oh, Caroline, Caroline, child of the sun,

There are battles with Fate that can never be won!

The star-flowering banner must never be furled,

For its blossoms of light are the hope of the world!

Go, then, our rash sister! afar and aloof,

Run wild in the sunshine away from our roof;

But when your heart aches and your feet have grown sore,

Remember the pathway that leads to our door!

OLIVER WENDELL HOLMES SR

All Quiet Along the Potomac

"All quiet along the Potomac," they say,
"Except now and then a stray picket
Is shot, as he walks on his beat to and fro,
By a rifleman hid in the thicket.
'T is nothing – a private or two now and then
Will not count in the news of the battle;
Not an officer lost – only one of the men,
Moaning out, all alone, the death-rattle."

All quiet along the Potomac to-night,
Where the soldiers lie peacefully dreaming;
Their tents in the rays of the clear autumn moon,
Or the light of the watch-fire, are gleaming.
A tremulous sigh of the gentle night-wind
Through the forest leaves softly is creeping;
While stars up above, with their glittering eyes,
Keep guard, for the army is sleeping.

There's only the sound of the lone sentry's tread,

As he tramps from the rock to the fountain,

And thinks of the two in the low trundle-bed

Far away in the cot on the mountain.

His musket falls slack; his face, dark and grim,

Grows gentle with memories tender,

As he mutters a prayer for the children asleep,

For their mother; may Heaven defend her!

The moon seems to shine just as brightly as then,

That night, when the love yet unspoken

Leaped up to his lips – when low-murmured vows

Were pledged to be ever unbroken.

Then drawing his sleeve roughly over his eyes,

He dashes off tears that are welling,

And gathers his gun closer up to its place,

As if to keep down the heart-swelling.

He passes the fountain, the blasted pine-tree,

    The footstep is lagging and weary;

Yet onward he goes, through the broad belt of light,

    Toward the shade of the forest so dreary.

Hark! was it the night-wind that rustled the leaves?

    Was it moonlight so wondrously flashing?

It looked like a rifle... "Ha! Mary, good-bye!"

    The red life-blood is ebbing and plashing.

All quiet along the Potomac to-night;

    No sound save the rush of the river;

While soft falls the dew on the face of the dead –

    The picket's off duty forever!

ETHEL LYNN BEERS

Civil War

"Rifleman, shoot me a fancy shot
Straight at the heart of yon prowling vidette;
Ring me a ball in the glittering spot
That shines on his breast like an amulet!"

"Ah, captain! here goes for a fine-drawn bead,
There's music around when my barrel's in tune!"
Crack! went the rifle, the messenger sped,
And dead from his horse fell the ringing dragoon.

"Now, rifleman, steal through the bushes, and snatch
From your victim some trinket to handsel first blood;
A button, a loop, or that luminous patch
That gleams in the moon like a diamond stud!"

"O captain! I staggered, and sunk on my track,
When I gazed on the face of that fallen vidette,
For he looked so like you, as he lay on his back,
That my heart rose upon me, and masters me yet.

"But I snatched off the trinket, – this locket of gold;
An inch from the centre my lead broke its way,
Scarce grazing the picture, so fair to behold,
Of a beautiful lady in bridal array."

"Ha! rifleman, fling me the locket! – 'tis she.
My brother's young bride, and the fallen dragoon
Was her husband – Hush! soldier, 't was Heaven's decree,
We must bury him there, by the light of the moon!

"But hark! the far bugles their warnings unite;
War is a virtue – weakness a sin;
There's a lurking and loping around us tonight;
Load again, rifleman, keep your hand in!"

CHARLES DAWSON SHANLY

When I Was Small, A Woman Died

When I was small, a woman died.

To-day her only boy

Went up from the Potomac,

His face all victory,

To look at her; how slowly

The seasons must have turned

Till bullets clipt an angle,

And he passed quickly round!

If pride shall be in Paradise

I never can decide;

Of their imperial conduct,

No person testified.

But proud in apparition,

That woman and her boy

Pass back and forth before my brain,

As ever in the sky.

EMILY DICKINSON

The Cumberland

At anchor in Hampton Roads we lay,

On board of the Cumberland, sloop-of-war;

And at times from the fortress across the bay

The alarum of drums swept past,

Or a bugle blast

From the camp on the shore.

Then far away to the south uprose

A little feather of snow-white smoke,

And we knew that the iron ship of our foes

Was steadily steering its course

To try the force

Of our ribs of oak.

Down upon us heavily runs,

Silent and sullen, the floating fort;

Then comes a puff of smoke from her guns,

And leaps the terrible death,

With fiery breath,

From each open port.

We are not idle, but send her straight
Defiance back in a full broadside!
As hail rebounds from a roof of slate,
Rebounds our heavier hail
From each iron scale
Of the monster's hide.

"Strike your flag!" the rebel cries,
In his arrogant old plantation strain.
"Never!" our gallant Morris replies;
"It is better to sink than to yield!"
And the whole air pealed
With the cheers of our men.

Then, like a kraken huge and black,
She crushed our ribs in her iron grasp!
Down went the Cumberland all a wrack,
With a sudden shudder of death,
And the cannon's breath
For her dying gasp.

Next morn, as the sun rose over the bay,

Still floated our flag at the mainmast head.

Lord, how beautiful was thy day!

Every waft of the air

Was a whisper of prayer,

Or a dirge for the dead.

Ho! brave hearts that went down in the seas!

Ye are at peace in the troubled stream;

Ho! brave land! with hearts like these,

Thy flag, that is rent in twain,

Shall be one again,

And without a seam!

HENRY WADSWORTH LONGFELLOW

Shiloh: A Requiem

(April, 1862)

Skimming lightly, wheeling still,

The swallows fly low

Over the field in clouded days,

The forest-field of Shiloh –

Over the field where April rain

Solaced the parched ones stretched in pain

Through the pause of night

That followed the Sunday fight

Around the church of Shiloh –

The church so lone, the log-built one,

That echoed to many a parting groan

And natural prayer

Of dying foemen mingled there –

Foemen at morn, but friends at eve –

Fame or country least their care:

(What like a bullet can undeceive!)

But now they lie low,

While over them the swallows skim,

And all is hushed at Shiloh.

HERMAN MELVILLE

To Canaän!

A Song of the Six Hundred Thousand

Where are you going, soldiers,

With banner, gun, and sword?

We're marching South to Canaän

To battle for the Lord!

What Captain leads your armies

Along the rebel coasts?

The Mighty One of Israel,

His name is Lord of Hosts!

To Canaän, to Canaän

The Lord has led us forth,

To blow before the heathen walls

The trumpets of the North!

What flag is this you carry

Along the sea and shore?

The same our grandsires lifted up, –

The same our fathers bore!

In many a battle's tempest

It shed the crimson rain, –

What God has woven in His loom
Let no man rend in twain!
To Canaän, to Canaän
The Lord has led us forth,
To plant upon the rebel towers
The banners of the North!

What troop is this that follows,
All armed with picks and spades?
These are the swarthy bondsmen, —
The iron-skin brigades!
They'll pile up Freedom's breastwork,
They'll scoop out rebels' graves;
Who then will be their owner
And march them off for slaves?
To Canaän, to Canaän
The Lord has led us forth,
To strike upon the captive's chain
The hammers of the North.

What song is this you're singing?
The same that Israel sung
When Moses led the mighty choir,
And Miriam's timbrel rung!

To Canaän! To Canaän!

The priests and maidens cried;

To Canaän! To Canaän!

The people's voice replied.

To Canaän, to Canaän

The Lord has led us forth,

To thunder through its adder dens

The anthems of the North!

When Canaän's hosts are scattered,

And all her walls lie flat,

What follows next in order?

– The Lord will see to that!

We'll break the tyrant's sceptre, –

We'll build the people's throne, –

When half the world is Freedom's

Then all the world's our own!

To Canaän, to Canaän

The Lord has led us forth,

To sweep the rebel threshing-floors,

A whirlwind from the North!

OLIVER WENDELL HOLMES SR

Malvern Hill

(July, 1862)

Ye elms that wave on Malvern Hill
 In prime of morn and May,
Recall ye how McClellan's men
 Here stood at bay?
While deep within yon forest dim
 Our rigid comrades lay –
Some with the cartridge in their mouth,
Others with fixed arms lifted South –
 Invoking so
The cypress glades? Ah wilds of woe!

The spires of Richmond, late beheld
 Through rifts in musket-haze,
Were closed from view in clouds of dust
 On leaf-walled ways,
Where streamed our wagons in caravan;
 And the Seven Nights and Days
Of march and fast, retreat and fight,
Pinched our grimed faces to ghastly plight –

Does the elm wood

Recall the haggard beards of blood?

The battle-smoked flag, with stars eclipsed,

We followed (it never fell!) –

In silence husbanded our strength –

Received their yell;

Till on this slope we patient turned

With cannon ordered well;

Reverse we proved was not defeat;

But ah, the sod what thousands meet! –

Does Malvern Wood

Bethink itself, and muse and brood?

We elms of Malvern Hill

Remember every thing;

But sap the twig will fill:

Wag the world how it will,

Leaves must be green in Spring.

HERMAN MELVILLE

29

He Fought Like Those Who've Nought To Lose

He fought like those Who've nought to lose –
Bestowed Himself to Balls
As One who for a further Life
Had not a further Use –

Invited Death – with bold attempt –
But Death was Coy of Him
As Other Men, were Coy of Death –
To Him – to live – was Doom –

His Comrades, shifted like the Flakes
When Gusts reverse the Snow –
But He – was left alive Because
Of Greediness to die –

EMILY DICKINSON

Dirge for a Soldier

(September 1, 1862)

Close his eyes; his work is done!
What to him is friend or foeman,
Rise of moon, or set of sun,
Hand of man, or kiss of woman?
Lay him low, lay him low,
In the clover or the snow!
What cares he? he cannot know:
Lay him low!

As man may, he fought his fight,
Proved his truth by his endeavor;
Let him sleep in solemn night,
Sleep forever and forever.
Lay him low, lay him low,
In the clover or the snow!
What cares he? he cannot know:
Lay him low!

Fold him in his country's stars,

Roll the drum and fire the volley!

What to him are all our wars,

What but death-bemocking folly?

Lay him low, lay him low,

In the clover or the snow!

What cares he? he cannot know:

Lay him low!

Leave him to God's watching eye;

Trust him to the hand that made him.

Mortal love weeps idly by:

God alone has power to aid him.

Lay him low, lay him low,

In the clover or the snow!

What cares he? he cannot know:

Lay him low!

GEORGE HENRY BOKER

The Battle
Autumn of 1862

The flags of war like storm-birds fly,
The charging trumpets blow,
Yet rolls no thunder in the sky,
No earthquake strives below.

And, calm and patient, Nature keeps
Her ancient promise well,
Though o'er her bloom and greenness sweeps
The battle's breath of hell.

And still she walks in golden hours
Through harvest-happy farms,
And still she wears her fruits and flowers
Like jewels on her arms.

What mean the gladness of the plain,
This joy of eve and morn,
The mirth that shakes the beard of grain
And yellow locks of corn?

Oh, eyes may be full of tears,
And hearts with hate are hot;
But even-paced come round the years,
And Nature changes not.

She meets with smiles our bitter grief,
With songs our groans of pain;
She mocks with tint of flower and leaf
The war-field's crimson stain.

Still, in the cannon's pause, we hear
Her sweet thanksgiving-psalm;
Too near to God for doubt or fear,
She shares the eternal calm.

She knows the seed lies safe below
The fires that blast and burn;
For all the tears of blood we sow
She waits the rich return.

She sees with clearer eye than ours

The good of suffering born –

The hearts that blossom like her flowers,

And ripen like her corn.

Oh, give to us, in times like these,

The vision of her eyes;

And make her fields and fruited trees

Our golden prophecies.

Oh, give to us her finer ear,

Above this stormy din.

We too would hear the bells of cheer

Ring peace and freedom in.

JOHN GREENLEAF WHITTIER

The Wound-Dresser

1

An old man bending, I come, among new faces,

Years looking backward, resuming, in answer to children,

Come tell us, old man, as from young men

and maidens that love me;

Years hence of these scenes, of these furious passions,

these chances,

Of unsurpass'd heroes, (was one side so brave?

the other was equally brave;)

Now be witness again – paint the mightiest armies of earth;

Of those armies so rapid, so wondrous,

what saw you to tell us?

What stays with you latest and deepest? of curious panics,

Of hard-fought engagements, or sieges tremendous,

what deepest remains?

2

O maidens and young men I love, and that love me,

What you ask of my days, those the strangest and sudden

your talking recalls;

Soldier alert I arrive, after a long march,

cover'd with sweat and dust;

In the nick of time I come, plunge in the fight, loudly shout

in the rush of successful charge;

Enter the captur'd works... yet lo!

like a swift-running river, they fade;

Pass and are gone, they fade – I dwell not on

soldiers' perils or soldiers' joys;

(Both I remember well – many the hardships,

few the joys, yet I was content.)

But in silence, in dreams' projections,

While the world of gain and appearance and mirth goes on,

So soon what is over forgotten, and waves

wash the imprints off the sand,

In nature's reverie sad, with hinged knees returning,

I enter the doors – (while for you up there,

Whoever you are, follow me without noise,

and be of strong heart.)

3

Bearing the bandages, water and sponge,

Straight and swift to my wounded I go,

Where they lie on the ground, after the battle brought in;

Where their priceless blood reddens the grass, the ground;

Or to the rows of the hospital tent,

or under the roof'd hospital;

To the long rows of cots, up and down, each side, I return;

To each and all, one after another,

I draw near – not one do I miss;

An attendant follows, holding a tray –

he carries a refuse pail,

Soon to be fill'd with clotted rags and blood,

emptied and fill'd again.

I onward go, I stop,

With hinged knees and steady hand, to dress wounds;

I am firm with each – the pangs are sharp, yet unavoidable;

One turns to me his appealing eyes –

(poor boy! I never knew you,

Yet I think I could not refuse this moment to die for you,

if that would save you.)

4

On, on I go! – (open doors of time! open hospital doors!)

The crush'd head I dress, (poor crazed hand,

tear not the bandage away;)

The neck of the cavalry-man, with the bullet

through and through, I examine;

Hard the breathing rattles, quite glazed already the eye,

yet life struggles hard;

(Come, sweet death! be persuaded, O beautiful death!

In mercy come quickly.)

From the stump of the arm, the amputated hand,

I undo the clotted lint, remove the slough,

wash off the matter and blood;

Back on his pillow the soldier bends,

with curv'd neck, and side-falling head;

His eyes are closed, his face is pale,

(he dares not look on the bloody stump,

And has not yet look'd on it.)

I dress a wound in the side, deep, deep;

But a day or two more – for see,

the frame all wasted already, and sinking,

And the yellow-blue countenance see.

I dress the perforated shoulder,

the foot with the bullet wound,

Cleanse the one with a gnawing and putrid gangrene,

so sickening, so offensive,

While the attendant stands behind aside me,

holding the tray and pail.

I am faithful, I do not give out;

The fractur'd thigh, the knee, the wound in the abdomen,

These and more I dress with impassive hand –

(yet deep in my breast a fire, a burning flame.)

5

Thus in silence, in dreams' projections,

Returning, resuming, I thread my way through the hospitals;

The hurt and wounded I pacify with soothing hand,

I sit by the restless all the dark night – some are so young;

Some suffer so much – I recall the experience sweet and sad;

(Many a soldier's loving arms about this neck

have cross'd and rested,

Many a soldier's kiss dwells on these bearded lips.)

WALT WHITMAN

Boston Hymn

(Read in Music Hall, January 1, 1863)

The word of the Lord by night
To the watching Pilgrims came,
As they sat by the seaside,
And filled their hearts with flame.

God said, I am tired of kings,
I suffer them no more;
Up to my ear the morning brings
The outrage of the poor.

Think ye I made this ball
A field of havoc and war,
Where tyrants great and tyrants small
Might harry the weak and poor?

My angel, – his name is Freedom, –
Choose him to be your king;
He shall cut pathways east and west
And fend you with his wing.

Lo! I uncover the land
Which I hid of old time in the West,
As the sculptor uncovers the statue
When he has wrought his best;

I show Columbia, of the rocks
Which dip their foot in the seas
And soar to the air-borne flocks
Of clouds and the boreal fleece.

I will divide my goods;
Call in the wretch and slave:
None shall rule but the humble,
And none but Toil shall have.

I will have never a noble,
No lineage counted great;
Fishers and choppers and ploughmen
Shall constitute a state.

Go, cut down trees in the forest
And trim the straightest boughs;
Cut down trees in the forest
And build me a wooden house.

Call the people together,
The young men and the sires,
The digger in the harvest-field,
Hireling and him that hires;

And here in a pine state-house
They shall choose men to rule
In every needful faculty,
In church and state and school.

Lo, now! if these poor men
Can govern the land and sea
And make just laws below the sun,
As planets faithful be.

And ye shall succor men;
'Tis nobleness to serve;
Help them who cannot help again:
Beware from right to swerve.

I break your bonds and masterships,
And I unchain the slave:
Free be his heart and hand henceforth
As wind and wandering wave.

I cause from every creature

His proper good to flow:

As much as he is and doeth,

So much he shall bestow.

But, lay hands on another

To coin his labor and sweat,

He goes in pawn for his victim

For eternal years in debt.

To-day unbind the captive,

So only are ye unbound;

Lift up a people from the dust,

Trump of their rescue, sound!

Pay ransom to the owner

And fill the bag to the brim.

Who is the owner? The slave is owner,

And ever was. Pay him.

O North! give him beauty for rags,
And honor, O South! for his shame;
Nevada! coin thy golden crags
With Freedom's image and name.

Up! and the dusky race
That sat in darkness long, –
Be swift their feet as antelopes,
And as behemoth strong.

Come, East and West and North,
By races, as snow flakes,
And carry my purpose forth,
Which neither halts nor shakes.

My will fulfilled shall be,
For, in daylight or in dark,
My thunderbolt has eyes to see
His way home to the mark.

RALPH WALDO EMERSON

Missing

In the cool, sweet hush of a wooded nook,

Where the May buds sprinkle the green old mound,

And the winds and the birds and the limpid brook,

Murmur their dreams with a drowsy sound;

Who lies so still in the plushy moss,

With his pale cheek pressed on a breezy pillow,

Couched where the light and the shadows cross

Through the flickering fringe of the willow?

Who lies, alas!

So still, so chill, in the whispering grass?

A soldier clad in the Zouave dress,

A bright-haired man, with his lips apart,

One hand thrown up o'er his frank, dead face,

And the other clutching his pulseless heart,

Lies here in the shadows, cool and dim,

His musket swept by a trailing bough,

With a careless grace in each quiet limb,

And a wound on his manly brow

A wound, alas!

Whence the warm blood drips on the quiet grass.

The violets peer from their dusky beds

With a tearful dew in their great pure eyes;

The lilies quiver their shining heads,

Their pale lips full of a sad surprise;

And the lizard darts through the glistening fern –

And the squirrel rustles the branches hoary;

Strange birds fly out, with a cry, to bathe

Their wings in the sunset glory;

While the shadows pass

O'er the quiet face and the dewy grass.

God pity the bride who waits at home,

With her lily cheeks and her violet eyes,

Dreaming the sweet old dreams of love,

While her lover is walking in Paradise;

God strengthen her heart as the days go by,

And the long, drear nights of her vigil follow,

Nor bird, nor moon, nor whispering wind,

May breathe the tale of the hollow;

Alas! Alas!

The secret is safe with the woodland grass.

AUTHOR UNKNOWN

Cavalry Crossing a Ford

A line in long array, where they wind betwixt green islands;

They take a serpentine course – their arms flash in the sun –

Hark to the musical clank;

Behold the silvery river – in it the splashing horses, loitering,

stop to drink;

Behold the brown-faced men – each group, each person, a

picture – the negligent rest on the saddles;

Some emerge on the opposite bank – others are just entering

the ford – while,

Scarlet, and blue, and snowy white,

The guidon flags flutter gaily in the wind.

WALT WHITMAN

The Reveille

Hark! I hear the tramp of thousands,
And of arméd men the hum;
Lo! a nation's hosts have gathered
Round the quick-alarming drum, –
Saying, "Come,
Freemen, come!
Ere your heritage be wasted," said the quick-alarming drum.

"Let me of my heart take counsel:
War is not of life the sum;
Who shall stay and reap the harvest
When the autumn days shall come?"
But the drum
Echoed: "Come!
Death shall reap the braver harvest," said the solemn-
sounding drum.

"But when won the coming battle,
What of profit springs therefrom?
What if conquest, subjugation,

Even greater ills become?"

But the drum

Answered: "Come!

You must do the sum to prove it," said the

Yankee-answering drum.

"What if, 'mid the cannons' thunder,

Whistling shot and bursting bomb

When my brothers fall around me,

Should my heart grow cold and numb?"

But the drum

Answered: "Come!

Better there in death united than in life a recreant, – Come!"

Thus they answered – hoping, fearing,

Some in faith, and doubting some,

Till a trumpet-voice proclaiming,

Said: "My chosen people, come!"

Then the drum,

Lo! was dumb;

For the great heart of the nation, throbbing, answered:

"Lord, we come!"

BRET HARTE

Gettysburg

There was no union in the land,
Though wise men labored long
With links of clay and ropes of sand
To bind the right and wrong.

There was no temper in the blade
That once could cleave a chain;
Its edge was dull with touch of trade
And clogged with rust of gain.

The sand and clay must shrink away
Before the lava tide:
By blows and blood and fire assay
The metal must be tried.

Here sledge and anvil met, and when
The furnace fiercest roared,
God's undiscerning workingmen
Reforged His people's sword.

Enough for them to ask and know
The moment's duty clear –
The bayonets flashed it there below,
The guns proclaimed it here:

To do and dare, and die at need,
But while life lasts, to fight –
For right or wrong a simple creed,
But simplest for the right.

They faltered not who stood that day
And held this post of dread;
Nor cowards they who wore the gray
Until the gray was red.

For every wreath the victor wears
The vanquished half may claim;
And every monument declares
A common pride and fame.

We raise no altar stones to Hate,
Who never bowed to Fear:
No province crouches at our gate,
To shame our triumph here.

Here standing by a dead wrong's grave

The blindest now may see,

The blow that liberates the slave

But sets the master free!

When ills beset the nation's life

Too dangerous to bear,

The sword must be the surgeon's knife,

Too merciful to spare.

O Soldier of our common land,

'Tis thine to bear that blade

Loose in the sheath, or firm in hand,

But ever unafraid.

When foreign foes assail our right,

One nation trusts to thee –

To wield it well in worthy fight –

The sword of Meade and Lee!

JAMES JEFFREY ROCHE

It Feels A Shame To Be Alive

It feels a shame to be Alive –
When Men so brave – are dead –
One envies the Distinguished Dust –
Permitted – such a Head –

The Stone – that tells defending Whom
This Spartan put away
What little of Him we – possessed
In Pawn for Liberty –

The price is great – Sublimely paid –
Do we deserve – a Thing –
That lives – like Dollars – must be piled
Before we may obtain?

Are we that wait – sufficient worth –

That such Enormous Pearl

As life – dissolved be – for Us –

In Battle's – horrid Bowl?

It may be – a Renown to live –

I think the Man who die –

Those unsustained – Saviors –

Present Divinity –

EMILY DICKINSON

The Thousand and Thirty-Seven

Three years ago, to-day,
We raised our hands to Heaven,
And, on the rolls of muster,
Our names were thirty-seven;
There were just a thousand bayonets,
And the swords were thirty-seven,
As we took our oath of service
With our right hands raised to Heaven.

Oh, 't was a gallant day,
In memory still adored.
That day of our sun-bright nuptials
With the musket and the sword!
Shrill rang the fifes, the bugles blared,
And beneath a cloudless heaven
Far flashed a thousand bayonets,
And the swords were thirty-seven.

Of the thousand stalwart bayonets
Two hundred march to-day;
Hundreds lie in Virginia swamps,

And hundreds in Maryland clay;
While other hundreds – less happy – drag
Their mangled limbs around,
And envy the deep, calm, blessed sleep
Of the battle-field's holy ground.

For the swords – one night a week ago,
The remnant, just eleven –
Gathered around a banqueting-board
With seats for thirty-seven.
There were two came in on crutches,
And two had each but a hand,
To pour the wine and raise the cup
As we toasted "Our Flag and Land!"

And the room seemed filled with whispers
As we looked at the vacant seats,
And with choking throats we pushed aside
The rich but untasted meats;
Then in silence we brimmed our glasses
As we stood up – just eleven –
And bowed as we drank to the Loved and the Dead
Who had made us thirty-seven!

PRIVATE MILES O'REILLY

A Dirge for McPherson

Killed in Front of Atlanta

(July 22, 1864)

Arms reversed and banners craped –
Muffled drums;
Snowy horses sable-draped –
McPherson comes.
But, tell us, shall we know him more,
Lost-Mountain and lone Kenesaw?

Brace the sword upon the pall –
A gleam in gloom;
So a bright name lighteth all
McPherson's doom.

Bear him through the chapel-door –
Let priest in stole
Pace before the warrior
Who led. Bell – toll!

Lay him down within the nave,

The Lesson read –

Man is noble, man is brave,

But man's – a weed.

Take him up again and wend

Graveward, nor weep:

There's a trumpet that shall rend

This Soldier's sleep.

Pass the ropes the coffin round,

And let descend;

Prayer and volley – let it sound

McPherson's end.

True fame is his, for life is o'er –

Sarpedon of the mighty war.

HERMAN MELVILLE

The Artilleryman's Vision

While my wife at my side lies slumbering, and the
wars are over long,
And my head on the pillow rests at home, and the
vacant midnight passes,
And through the stillness, through the dark, I hear,
just hear, the breath of my infant,
There in the room, as I wake from sleep,
this vision presses upon me:
The engagement opens there and then, in fantasy unreal;
The skirmishers begin – they crawl cautiously ahead –
I hear the irregular snap! snap!
I hear the sounds of the different missiles –
the short *t-h-t! t-h-t!* of the rifle balls;
I see the shells exploding, leaving small white clouds –
I hear the great shells shrieking as they pass;
The grape, like the hum and whirr of wind through the trees,
(quick, tumultuous, now the contest rages!)
All the scenes at the batteries themselves rise
in detail before me again;

The crashing and smoking – the pride of the
men in their pieces;
The chief gunner ranges and sights his piece,
and selects a fuse of the right time;
After firing, I see him lean aside, and look eagerly
off to note the effect;
– Elsewhere I hear the cry of a regiment charging –
(the young colonel leads himself this time,
with brandish'd sword;)
I see the gaps cut by the enemy's volleys,
(quickly fill'd up, no delay;)
I breathe the suffocating smoke –
then the flat clouds hover low, concealing all;
Now a strange lull comes for a few seconds,
not a shot fired on either side;
Then resumed, the chaos louder than ever,
with eager calls, and orders of officers;
While from some distant part of the field the wind wafts to
my ears a shout of applause, (some special success;)

And ever the sound of the cannon, far or near,

(rousing, even in dreams, a devilish exultation, and all the

old mad joy, in the depths of my soul;)

And ever the hastening of infantry shifting positions –

batteries, cavalry, moving hither and thither;

(The falling, dying, I heed not – the wounded, dripping and

red, I heed not – some to the rear are hobbling;)

Grime, heat, rush – aid-de-camps galloping by,

or on a full run;

With the patter of small arms, the warning *s-s-t* of the rifles,

(these in my vision I hear or see,)

And bombs busting in air, and at night the vari-color'd

rockets.

WALT WHITMAN

Sheridan's Ride

(October 19, 1864)

Up from the South, at break of day,

Bringing to Winchester fresh dismay,

The affrighted air with a shudder bore,

Like a herald in haste to the chieftain's door,

The terrible grumble, and rumble, and roar,

Telling the battle was on once more,

And Sheridan twenty miles away.

And wider still those billows of war

Thundered along the horizon's bar;

And louder yet into Winchester rolled

The roar of that red sea uncontrolled.

Making the blood of the listener cold,

As he thought of the stake in that fiery fray,

With Sheridan twenty miles away.

But there is a road from Winchester town,

A good, broad highway leading down:

And there, through the flush of the morning light,

A steed as black as the steeds of night

Was seen to pass, as with eagle flight;

As if he knew the terrible need,

He stretched away with his utmost speed.

Hills rose and fell, but his heart was gay,

With Sheridan fifteen miles away.

Still sprang from those swift hoofs, thundering south,

The dust like smoke from the cannon's mouth,

Or the trail of a comet, sweeping faster and faster,

Foreboding to traitors the doom of disaster.

The heart of the steed and the heart of the master

Were beating like prisoners assaulting their walls,

Impatient to be where the battle-field calls:

Every nerve of the charger was strained to full play,

With Sheridan only ten miles away.

Under his spurning feet, the road
Like an arrowy Alpine river flowed,
And the landscape sped away behind
Like an ocean flying before the wind;
And the steed, like a bark fed with furnace ire,
Swept on, with his wild eye full of fire;
But, lo! he is nearing his heart's desire;
He is snuffing the smoke of the roaring fray,
With Sheridan only five miles away.

The first that the general saw were the groups
Of stragglers, and then the retreating troops;
What was done? what to do? a glance told him both.
Then striking his spurs with a terrible oath,
He dashed down the line, 'mid a storm of huzzas,
And the wave of retreat checked its course there, because
The sight of the master compelled it to pause.
With foam and with dust the black charger was gray:
By the flash of his eye, and the red nostril's play,
He seemed to the whole great army to say:
"I have brought you Sheridan all the way
From Winchester down to save the day."

Hurrah! hurrah for Sheridan!

Hurrah! hurrah for horse and man!

And when their statues are placed on high

Under the dome of the Union sky,

The American soldier's Temple of Fame,

There, with the glorious general's name,

Be it said, in letters both bold and bright:

"Here is the steed that saved the day

By carrying Sheridan into the fight,

From Winchester – twenty miles away!"

THOMAS BUCHANAN READ

Vigil Strange I Kept on the Field One Night

Vigil strange I kept on the field one night:

When you, my son and my comrade, dropt at my side that day,

One look I but gave, which your dear eyes return'd,

with a look I shall never forget;

One touch of your hand to mine, O boy, reach'd up as you

lay on the ground;

Then onward I sped in the battle, the even-contested battle;

Till late in the night reliev'd, to the place at last again

I made my way;

Found you in death so cold, dear comrade – found your body, son

of responding kisses, (never again on earth responding;)

Bared your face in the starlight – curious the scene –

cool blew the moderate night-wind;

Long there and then in vigil I stood, dimly around me the

battle-field spreading;

Vigil wondrous and vigil sweet, there in the fragrant silent night;

But not a tear fell, not even a long-drawn sigh – Long, long I gazed;

Then on the earth partially reclining, sat by your side,

leaning my chin in my hands;

Passing sweet hours, immortal and mystic hours with you, dearest
comrade – Not a tear, not a word;
Vigil of silence, love and death – vigil for you my son
and my soldier,
As onward silently stars aloft, eastward new ones upward stole;
Vigil final for you, brave boy, (I could not save you,
swift was your death,
I faithfully loved you and cared for you living –
I think we shall surely meet again;)
Till at latest lingering of the night, indeed just
as the dawn appear'd,
My comrade I wrapt in his blanket, envelop'd well his form,
Folded the blanket well, tucking it carefully over head, and
carefully under feet;
And there and then, and bathed by the rising sun, my son in his
grave, in his rude-dug grave I deposited;

Ending my vigil strange with that – vigil of night and

battlefield dim;

Vigil for boy of responding kisses,

(never again on earth responding;)

Vigil for comrade swiftly slain – vigil I never forget,

how as day brighten'd,

I rose from the chill ground, and folded my

soldier well in his blanket,

And buried him where he fell.

WALT WHITMAN

Christmas Bells

I heard the bells on Christmas Day
Their old familiar carols play,
And wild and sweet
The words repeat
Of peace on earth, good-will to men!

And thought how, as the day had come,
The belfries of all Christendom
Had rolled along
The unbroken song
Of peace on earth, good-will to men!

Till, ringing, singing on its way,
The world revolved from night to day,
A voice, a chime
A chant sublime
Of peace on earth, good-will to men!

Then from each black, accursed mouth

The cannon thundered in the South,

And with the sound

The carols drowned

Of peace on earth, good-will to men!

It was as if an earthquake rent

The hearth-stones of a continent,

And made forlorn

The households born

Of peace on earth, good-will to men!

And in despair I bowed my head;

"There is no peace on earth," I said;

"For hate is strong,

And mocks the song

Of peace on earth, good-will to men!"

Then pealed the bells more loud and deep:

"God is not dead; nor doth he sleep!

The Wrong shall fail,

The Right prevail,

Of peace on earth, good-will to men!"

HENRY WADSWORTH LONGFELLOW

Laus Deo!

It is done!
Clang of bell and roar of gun
Send the tidings up and down.
How the belfries rock and reel!
How the great guns, peal on peal,
Fling the joy from town to town!

Ring, O bells!
Every stroke exulting tells
Of the burial hour of crime.
Loud and long, that all may hear,
Ring for every listening ear
Of Eternity and Time!

Let us kneel:

God's own voice is in that peal,

And this spot is holy ground.

Lord, forgive us! What are we,

That our eyes this glory see,

That our ears have heard the sound!

For the Lord

On the whirlwind is abroad;

In the earthquake He has spoken;

He has smitten with His thunder

The iron walls asunder,

And the gates of brass are broken!

Loud and long

Lift the old exulting song;

Sing with Miriam by the sea,

He has cast the mighty down;

Horse and rider sink and drown;

"He hath triumphed gloriously!"

Did we dare,

In our agony of prayer,

Ask for more than He has done?

When was ever His right hand

Over any time or land

Stretched as now beneath the sun?

How they pale,

Ancient myth and song and tale,

In this wonder of our days,

When the cruel rod of war

Blossoms white with righteous law,

And the wrath of man is praise!

Blotted out!

All within and all about

Shall a fresher life begin;

Freer breathe the universe

As it rolls its heavy curse

On the dead and buried sin!

It is done!

In the circuit of the sun

Shall the sound thereof go forth.

It shall bid the sad rejoice,

It shall give the dumb a voice,

It shall belt with joy the earth!

Ring and swing,

Bells of joy! On morning's wing

Send the song of praise abroad!

With a sound of broken chains

Tell the nations that He reigns,

Who alone is Lord and God!

JOHN GREENLEAF WHITTIER

Spirit Whose Work is Done

Spirit whose work is done! spirit of dreadful hours!

Ere, departing, fade from my eyes your forests of bayonets;

Spirit of gloomiest fears and doubts, (yet onward ever

unfaltering pressing;)

Spirit of many a solemn day, and many a savage scene!

Electric spirit!

That with muttering voice, through the war now closed,

like a tireless phantom flitted,

Rousing the land with breath of flame,

while you beat and beat the drum;

– Now, as the sound of the drum,

hollow and harsh to the last, reverberates round me;

As your ranks, your immortal ranks,

return, return from the battles;

While the muskets of the young men yet

lean over their shoulders;

While I look on the bayonets bristling over their shoulders;

While those slanted bayonets, whole forests of them,

appearing in the distance, approach and pass on,

returning homeward,

Moving with steady motion, swaying to and fro,

to the right and left,

Evenly, lightly rising and falling, as the steps keep time;

– Spirit of hours I knew, all hectic red one day,

but pale as death next day;

Touch my mouth, ere you depart – press my lips close!

Leave me your pulses of rage! bequeath them to me!

fill me with currents convulsive!

Let them scorch and blister out of my chants,

when you are gone;

Let them identify you to the future, in these songs.

WALT WHITMAN

My Portion is Defeat To-day

My portion is defeat to-day,

A paler luck than victory,

Less paeans, fewer bells –

The drums don't follow me with tunes,

Defeat a something dumber means,

More difficult than bells.

'Tis populous with bone and stain,

And men too straight to bend again,

And piles of solid moan,

And chips of blank in boyish eyes,

And shreds of prayer and death's surprise

Stamped visible in stone.

There's something prouder over there –

The trumpets tell it in the air.

How different victory to him

Who has it, and the One

Who to have had it would have been

Contenteder to die.

EMILY DICKINSON

O Captain! My Captain!

O Captain! my Captain! our fearful trip is done;

The ship has weather'd every rack, the prize

we sought is won;

The port is near, the bells I hear, the people all exulting,

While follow eyes the steady keel, the vessel grim and

daring:

But O heart, heart, heart!

O the bleeding drops of red,

Where on the deck my Captain lies,

Fallen cold and dead.

O Captain! my Captain! rise up and hear the bells;

Rise up – for you the flag is flung – for you the bugle trills;

For you bouquets and ribbon'd wreaths –

for you the shores a-crowding;

For you they call, the swaying mass, their eager faces

turning;

Here Captain, dear father!

This arm beneath your head;

It is some dream that on the deck,

You've fallen cold and dead.

My Captain does not answer, his lips are pale and still;

My father does not feel my arm, he has no pulse nor will;

The ship is anchor'd safe and sound, its voyage closed and

done;

From fearful trip, the victor ship, comes in with object won;

Exult, O shores, and ring, O bells!

But I, with mournful tread,

Walk the deck my Captain lies,

Fallen cold and dead.

WALT WHITMAN

The Martyr

(Indicative of the Passion of the People on the 15th day of April, 1865)

Good Friday was the day
Of the prodigy and crime,
When they killed him in his pity,
When they killed him in his prime
Of clemency and calm –
When with yearning he was filled
To redeem the evil-willed,
And, though conqueror, be kind;
But they killed him in his kindness,
In their madness and their blindness,
And they killed him from behind.

There is sobbing of the strong,
And a pall upon the land;
But the People in their weeping
Bare the iron hand;
Beware the People weeping
When they bare the iron hand.

He lieth in his blood –

The father in his face;

They have killed him, the Forgiver –

The Avenger takes his place,

The Avenger wisely stern,

Who in righteousness shall do

What the heavens call him to,

And the parricides remand;

For they killed him in his kindness,

In their madness and their blindness,

And his blood is on their hand.

There is sobbing of the strong,

And a pall upon the land;

But the People in their weeping

Bare the iron hand;

Beware the People weeping

When they bare the iron hand.

HERMAN MELVILLE

Reconciliation

Word over all, beautiful as the sky!

Beautiful that war, and all its deeds of carnage, must in time

be utterly lost;

That the hands of the sisters Death and Night, incessantly

softly wash again, and ever again, this soil'd world:

… For my enemy is dead – a man divine as myself is dead;

I look where he lies, white-faced and still, in the coffin – I

draw near;

I bend down, and touch lightly with my lips the white face in

the coffin.

WALT WHITMAN

To E.S. Salomon

*Who in a Memorial Day oration protested bitterly against
decorating the graves of Confederate dead.*

What! Salomon! such words from you,
Who call yourself a soldier? Well,
The Southern brother where he fell
Slept all your base oration through.

Alike to him – he cannot know
Your praise or blame: as little harm
Your tongue can do him as your arm
A quarter-century ago.

The brave respect the brave. The brave
Respect the dead; but *you* – you draw
That ancient blade, the ass's jaw,
And shake it o'er a hero's grave.

Are you not he who makes to-day
A merchandise of old renown
Which he persuades this easy town
He won in battle far away?

Nay, those the fallen who revile
Have ne'er before the living stood
And stoutly made their battle good
And greeted danger with a smile.

What if the dead whom still you hate
Were wrong? Are you so surely right?
We know the issues of the fight –
The sword is but an advocate.

Men live and die, and other men
Arise with knowledges diverse:
What seemed a blessing seems a curse,
And Now is still at odds with Then.

The years go on, the old comes back
To mock the new – beneath the sun
Is *nothing* new; ideas run
Recurrent in an endless track.

What most we censure, men as wise
Have reverently practised; nor
Will future wisdom fail to war
On principles we dearly prize.

We do not know – we can but deem,
And he is loyalest and best
Who takes the light full on his breast
And follows it throughout the dream.

The broken light, the shadows wide –
Behold the battle-field displayed!
God save the vanquished from the blade,
The victor from the victor's pride.

If, Salomon, the blessed dew
That falls upon the Blue and Gray
Is powerless to wash away
The sin of differing from you,

Remember how the flood of years
Has rolled across the erring slain;
Remember, too, the cleansing rain
Of widows' and of orphans' tears.

The dead are dead – let that atone:
And though with equal hand we strew
The blooms on saint and sinner too,
Yet God will know to choose his own.

The wretch, whate'er his life and lot,
Who does not love the harmless dead
With all his heart and all his head –
May God forgive him, *I* shall not.

When, Salomon, you come to quaff
The Darker Cup with meeker face,
I, loving you at last, shall trace
Upon your tomb this epitaph:

"Draw near, ye generous and brave –
Kneel round this monument and weep
For one who tried in vain to keep
A flower from a soldier's grave."

AMBROSE BIERCE

Robert E. Lee

A gallant foeman in the fight,
A brother when the fight was o'er,
The hand that led the host with might
The blessed torch of learning bore.

No shriek of shells nor roll of drums,
No challenge fierce, resounding far,
When reconciling Wisdom comes
To heal the cruel wounds of war.

Thought may the minds of men divide,
Love makes the heart of nations one,
And so, the soldier grave beside,
We honor thee, Virginia's son.

JULIA WARD HOWE

A Year's "Casualties"

Slain as they lay by the secret, slow,

Pitiless hand of an unseen foe,

Two score thousand old soldiers have crossed

The river to join the loved and lost.

In the space of a year their spirits fled,

Silent and white, to the camp of the dead.

One after one they fall asleep

And the pension agents awake to weep,

And orphaned statesmen are loud in their wail

As the souls flit by on the evening gale.

O Father of Battles, pray give us release

From the horrors of peace, the horrors of peace!

AMBROSE BIERCE

The Blue and The Gray

By the flow of the inland river,
Whence the fleets of iron have fled,
Where the blades of the grave-grass quiver,
Asleep are the ranks of the dead:
Under the sod and the dew,
Waiting the judgment-day;
Under the one, the Blue,
Under the other, the Gray.

These in the robings of glory,
Those in the gloom of defeat,
All with the battle-blood gory,
In the dusk of eternity meet:
Under the sod and the dew,
Waiting the judgment-day;
Under the laurel, the Blue,
Under the willow, the Gray.

From the silence of sorrowful hours

The desolate mourners go,

Lovingly laden with flowers

Alike for the friend and the foe:

Under the sod and the dew,

Waiting the judgment-day;

Under the roses, the Blue,

Under the lilies, the Gray.

So with an equal splendor,

The morning sunrays fall,

With a touch impartially tender,

On the blossoms blooming for all:

Under the sod and the dew,

Waiting the judgment-day;

Broidered with gold, the Blue,

Mellowed with gold, the Gray.

So, when the summer calleth,

On forest and field of grain,

With an equal murmur falleth

The cooling drip of the rain:

Under the sod and the dew,

Waiting the judgment-day;

Wet with the rain, the Blue,

Wet with the rain, the Gray.

Sadly, but not with upbraiding,

The generous deed was done,

In the storm of the years that are fading

No braver battle was won:

Under the sod and the dew,

Waiting the judgment-day;

Under the blossoms, the Blue,

Under the garlands, the Gray.

No more shall the war-cry sever,

Or the winding rivers be red;

They banish our anger forever

When they laurel the graves of our dead!

Under the sod and the dew,

Waiting the judgment-day;

Love and tears for the Blue,

Tears and love for the Gray.

FRANCIS MILES FINCH

THE GRAY

Over the River

We hail your "Stripes" and lessened "Stars,"

As one may hail a neighbor;

Now forward move! no fear of jars,

With nothing but free labor;

And we will mind our slaves and farm,

And never wish you any harm,

But greet you – over the river.

The self-same language do we speak,

The same dear words we utter;

Then let's not make each other weak,

Nor 'gainst each other mutter;

But let each go his separate way,

And each will doff his hat, and say:

"I greet you – over the river!"

Our flags, almost the same, unfurl,
And nod across the border;
Ohio's waves between them curl –
Our stripe's a little broader;
May yours float out on every breeze,
And, in our wake, traverse all seas –
We greet you – over the river!

We part as friends of years should part,
With pleasant words and wishes,
And no desire is in our heart
For Lincoln's loaves and fishes:
"Farewell," we wave you from afar,
We like you best – just where you are –
And greet you – over the river!

JANE T.H. CROSS

Farewell to Brother Jonathan

Farewell! we must part; we have turned from the land
Of our cold-hearted brother, with tyrannous hand,
Who assumed all our rights as a favor to grant,
And whose smile ever covered the sting of a taunt;

Who breathed on the fame he was bound to defend, –
Still the craftiest foe, 'neath the guise of a friend;
Who believed that our bosoms would bleed at a touch,
Yet could never believe he could goad them too much;

Whose conscience affects to be seared with our sin,
Yet is plastic to take all its benefits in;
The mote in our eye so enormous has grown,
That he never perceived there's a beam in his own.

O Jonathan, Jonathan! vassal of pelf,
Self-righteous, self-glorious, yes, every inch self,
Your loyalty now is all bluster and boast,
But was dumb when the foemen invaded our coast.

In vain did your country appeal to you then,

You coldly refused her your money and men;

Your trade interrupted, you slunk from her wars,

And preferred British gold to the Stripes and the Stars!

Then our generous blood was as water poured forth,

And the sons of the South were the shields of the North;

Nor our patriot ardor one moment gave o'er,

Till the foe you had fed we had driven from the shore!

Long years we have suffered opprobrium and wrong,

But we clung to your side with affection so strong,

That at last, in mere wanton aggression, you broke

All the ties of our hearts with one murderous stroke.

We are tired of contest for what is our own,

We are sick of a strife that could never be done;

Thus our love has died out, and its altars are dark,

Not Prometheus's self could rekindle the spark.

O Jonathan, Jonathan! deadly the sin,

Of your tigerish thirst for the blood of your kin;

And shameful the spirit that gloats over wives

And maidens despoiled of their honor and lives!

Your palaces rise from the fruits of our toil,

Your millions are fed from the wealth of our soil;

The balm of our air brings the health to your cheek;

And our hearts are aglow with the welcome we speak.

O brother! beware how you seek us again,

Lest you brand on your forehead the signet of Cain;

That blood and that crime on your conscience must sit;

We may fall – we may perish – but never submit!

The pathway that leads to the Pharisee's door

We remember, indeed, but we tread it no more;

Preferring to turn, with the Publican's faith,

To the path through the valley and shadow of death!

CAROLINE

Carolina

I

The despot treads thy sacred sands,

Thy pines give shelter to his bands

Thy sons stand by with idle hands

Carolina!

He breathes at ease thy airs of balm,

He scorns the lances of thy palm;

Oh! who shall break thy craven calm,

Carolina!

Thy ancient fame is growing dim,

A spot is on thy garment's rim;

Give to the winds thy battle hymn,

Carolina!

II

Call thy children of the hill,

Wake swamp and river, coast and rill,

Rouse all thy strength and all thy skill,

Carolina!

Cite wealth and science, trade and art,

Touch with thy fire the cautious mart,

And pour thee through the people's heart,

Carolina!

Till even the coward spurns his fears,

And all thy fields and fens and meres

Shall bristle like thy palm with spears,

Carolina!

III

Hold up the glories of thy dead;

Say how thy elder children bled,

And point to Eutaw's battle bed,

Carolina!

Tell how the patriot's soul was tried,

And what his dauntless breast defied;

How Rutledge ruled and Laurens died,

Carolina!

Cry! till thy summons, heard at last,

Shall fall like Marion's bugle-blast

Re-echoed from the haunted Past,

Carolina!

IV

I hear a murmur as of waves

That grope their way through sunless caves,

Like bodies struggling in their graves,

Carolina!

And now it deepens; slow and grand

It swells, as rolling to the land,

An ocean broke upon the strand,

Carolina!

Shout! let it reach the startled Huns!

And roar with all thy festal guns!

It is the answer of thy sons,

Carolina!

V

They will not wait to hear thee call;

From Sachem's Head to Sumter's wall

Resounds the voice of hut and hall,

Carolina!

No! thou hast not a stain, they say,

Or none save what the battle-day

Shall wash in seas of blood away,

Carolina!

Thy skirts indeed the foe may part,

Thy robe be pierced with sword and dart,

They shall not touch thy noble heart,

Carolina!

VI

Ere thou shalt own the tyrant's thrall

Ten times ten thousand men must fall;

Thy corpse may hearken to his call,

Carolina!

When, by thy bier, in mournful throngs

The women chant thy mortal wrongs,

'Twill be their own funereal songs,

Carolina!

From thy dead breast by ruffians trod

No helpless child shall look to God;

All shall be safe beneath thy sod,

Carolina!

VII

Girt with such wills to do and bear,

Assured in right, and mailed in prayer.

Thou wilt not bow thee to despair,

Carolina!

Throw thy bold banner to the breeze!

Front with thy ranks the threatening seas

Like thine own proud armorial trees,

Carolina!

Fling down thine gauntlet to the Huns,

And roar the challenge from thy guns;

Then leave the future to thy sons,

Carolina!

HENRY TIMROD

Wouldst Thou Have Me Love Thee?

Wouldst thou have me love thee, dearest,

With a woman's proudest heart,

Which shall ever hold thee nearest,

Shrined in its inmost part?

Listen, then! My country's calling

On her sons to meet the foe!

Leave these groves of rose and myrtle;

Drop thy dreamy harp of love!

Like young Korner – scorn the turtle,

When the eagle screams above!

Dost thou pause? – Let dastards dally –

Do thou for thy country fight!

'Neath her noble emblem rally –

"God, our country, and our right!"

Listen! now her trumpet's calling

On her sons to meet the foe!

Woman's heart is soft and tender,

But 'tis proud and faithful, too;

Shall she be her land's defender?

Lover! Soldier! up and do!

Seize thy father's ancient falchion,

Which once flashed as freedom's star!

Till sweet peace – the bow and halycon,

Stilled the stormy strife of war.

Listen! now their country's calling

On her sons to meet her foe!

Sweet is love in moonlight bowers!

Sweet the altar and the flame!

Sweet the spring-time with her flowers!

Sweeter far the patriot's name!

Should the God who smiles above thee,

Doom thee to a soldier's grave,

Hearts will break, but fame will love thee,

Canonized among the brave!

Listen, then! thy country's calling

On her sons to meet the foe!

Rather would I view thee lying

On the last red field of strife,

'Mid thy country's heroes dying,

Than become a dastard's wife!

ALEXANDER B. MEEK

Charleston

Calm as that second summer which precedes
The first fall of the snow,
In the broad sunlight of heroic deeds
The city bides the foe.

As yet, behind their ramparts stern and proud,
Her bolted thunders sleep –
Dark Sumter, like a battlemented cloud,
Looms o'er the solemn deep.

No Calpe frowns from lofty cliff or scar
To guard the holy strand;
But Moultrie holds in leash her dogs of war
Above the level sand.

And down the dunes a thousand guns lie couched,
Unseen, beside the flood –
Like tigers in some Orient jungle crouched
That wait and watch for blood.

Meanwhile, through streets still echoing with trade,
  Walk grave and thoughtful men,
Whose hands may one day wield the patriot's blade
  As lightly as the pen.

And maidens, with such eyes as would grow dim
  Over a bleeding hound,
Seem each one to have caught the strength of him
  Whose sword she sadly bound.

Thus girt without and garrisoned at home,
  Day patient following day,
Old Charleston looks from roof, and spire, and dome,
  Across her tranquil bay.

Ships, through a hundred foes, from Saxon lands
  And spicy Indian ports,
Bring Saxon steel and iron to her hands,
  And Summer to her courts.

But still, along yon dim Atlantic line,

The only hostile smoke

Creeps like a harmless mist above the brine,

From some frail, floating oak.

Shall the Spring dawn, and she still clad in smiles,

And with an unscathed brow,

Rest in the strong arms of her palm-crowned isles,

As fair and free as now?

We know not; in the temple of the Fates

God has inscribed her doom;

And, all untroubled in her faith, she waits

The triumph or the tomb.

HENRY TIMROD

The Virginians of the Valley

The knightliest of the knightly race
That, since the days of old,
Have kept the lamp of chivalry
Alight in hearts of gold:
The kindliest of the kindly band
That, rarely hating ease,
Yet rode with Spotswood round the land,
And Raleigh round the seas;

Who climbed the blue Virginian hills
Against embattled foes,
And planted there, in valleys fair,
The lily and the rose;
Whose fragrance lives in many lands,
Whose beauty stars the earth,
And lights the hearths of happy homes
With loveliness and worth.

We thought they slept! – the sons who kept

The names of noble sires,

And slumbered while the darkness crept

Around their vigil-fires;

But aye the "Golden Horseshoe" knights

Their old Dominion keep,

Whose foes have found enchanted ground,

But not a knight asleep!

FRANCIS ORRAY TICKNOR

Albert Sidney Johnston

I hear again the tread of war go thundering through the land,
And Puritan and Cavalier are clinching neck and hand,
Round Shiloh church the furious foes have met to thrust and slay,
Where erst the peaceful sons of Christ were wont to kneel and pray.

The wrestling of the ages shakes the hills of Tennessee,
With all their echoing mounts a-throb with war's wild minstrelsy;
A galaxy of stars new-born round the shield of Mars,
And set against the Stars and Stripes the flashing Stars and Bars.

'Twas Albert Sidney Johnston led the columns of the Gray,
Like Hector on the plains of Troy his presence fired the fray;
And dashing horse and gleaming sword spake out his royal will
As on the slopes of Shiloh field the blasts of war blew shrill.

"Down with the base invaders," the Gray shout forth the cry,
"Death to presumptuous rebels," the Blue ring out reply;
All day the conflict rages and yet again all day,
Though Grant is on the Union side he cannot stem nor stay.

They are a royal race of men, these brothers face to face,

Their fury speaking through their guns, their frenzy in their pace;

The sweeping onset of the Gray bears down the sturdy Blue,

Though Sherman and his legions are heroes through and through.

Though Prentiss and his gallant men are forcing scaur and crag,

They fall like sheaves before the scythes of Hardee and of Bragg;

Ah, who shall tell the victor's tale when all the strife is past,

When man and man in one great mould the men who strive are cast.

As when the Trojan hero came from that fair city's gates,

With tossing mane and flaming crest to scorn the scowling fates,

His legions gather round him and madly charge and cheer,

And fill the besieging armies with wild disheveled fear.

Then bares his breast unto the dart the daring spearsman sends,

And dying hears his cheering foes, the wailing of his friends,

So Albert Sidney Johnston, the chief of belt and scar,

Lay down to die at Shiloh and turned the scales of war.

Now five and twenty years are gone, and lo, today they come,

The Blue and Gray in proud array with throbbing fife and drum;

But not as rivals, not as foes, as brothers reconciled,

To twine love's fragrant roses where the thorns of hate grew wild.

They tell the hero of three wars, the lion-hearted man,

Who wore his valor like a star – uncrowned American;

Above his heart serene and still the folded Stars and Bars,

Above his head like mother-wings, the sheltering Stripes and Stars.

Aye, five and twenty years, and lo, the manhood of the South

Has held its valor stanch and strong as at the cannon's mouth,

With patient heart and silent tongue has kept its true parole,

And in the conquests born of peace has crowned its battle roll.

But ever while we sing of war, of courage tried and true,

Of heroes wed to gallant deeds, or be it Gray or Blue,

Then Albert Sidney Johnston's name shall flash before our sight

Like some resplendent meteor across the sombre night.

America, thy sons are knit with sinews wrought of steel,

They will not bend, they will not break, beneath the tyrant's heel;

But in the white-hot flame of love, to silken cobwebs spun,

They whirl the engines of the world, all keeping time as one.

Today they stand abreast and strong, who stood as foes of yore,

The world leaps up to bless their feet, heaven scatters blessings o'er;

Their robes are wrought of gleaming gold, their wings are

freedom's own,

The tramping of their conquering hosts shakes

pinnacle and throne.

Oh, veterans of the Blue and Gray, who fought on Shiloh field,

The purposes of God are true, His judgment stands revealed;

The pangs of war have rent the veil, and lo, His high decree;

One heart, one hope, one destiny, one flag from sea to sea.

KATE BROWNLEE SHERWOOD

The Lone Sentry

'Twas in the dying of the day,
The darkness grew so still;
The drowsy pipe of evening birds
Was hushed upon the hill;
Athwart the shadows of the vale
Slumbered the men of might,
And one lone sentry paced his rounds,
To watch the camp that night.

A grave and solemn man was he,
With deep and sombre brow,
The dreamful eyes seemed hoarding up
Some unaccomplished vow.
The wistful glance peered o'er the plains
Beneath the starry light,
And with the murmured name of God,
He watched the camp that night.

The Future opened unto him
Its grand and awful scroll:
Manassas and the Valley march

Came heaving o'er his soul;
Richmond and Sharpsburg thundered by
With that tremendous fight
Which gave him to the angel hosts
Who watched the camp that night.

We mourn for him who died for us
With one resistless moan;
While up the valley of the Lord
He marches to the Throne!
He kept the faith of men and saints
Sublime, and pure, and bright –
He sleeps – and all is well with him
Who watched the camp that night.

Brothers! the Midnight of the Cause
Is shrouded in our fate;
The demon Goths pollute our halls
With fire, and lust, and hate.
Be strong – be valiant – be assured –
Strike home for Heaven and Right!
The soul of Jackson stalks abroad,
And guards the camp tonight.

JAMES RYDER RANDALL

Manassas

They have met at last – as storm-clouds
Meet in heaven,
And the Northmen back and bleeding
Have been driven;
And their thunders have been stilled,
And their leaders crushed or killed,
And their ranks with terror thrilled,
Rent and riven!

Like the leaves of Valambrosa
They are lying;
In the moonlight, in the midnight,
Dead and dying;
Like those leaves before the gale,
Swept their legions, wild and pale;
While the host that made them quail
Stood, defying.

When aloft in morning sunlight

Flags were flaunted,

And "swift vengeance on the rebel"

Proudly vaunted:

Little did they think that night

Should close upon their shameful flight,

And rebels, victors in the fight,

Stand undaunted.

But peace to those who perished

In our passes!

Light be the earth above them;

Green the grasses!

Long shall Northmen rue the day

When they met our stern array,

And shrunk from battle's wild affray

At Manassas.

CATHERINE M. WARFIELD

The Bivouac in the Snow

Halt! – the march is over,
Day is almost done;
Loose the cumbrous knapsack,
Drop the heavy gun.
Chilled and wet and weary,
Wander to and fro,
Seeking wood to kindle
Fires amidst the snow.

Round the bright blaze gather,
Heed not sleet or cold;
Ye are Spartan soldiers,
Stout and brave and bold.
Never Xerxian army
Yet subdued a foe
Who but asked a blanket
On a bed of snow.

Shivering, 'midst the darkness,

Christian men are found,

There devoutly kneeling

On the frozen ground –

Pleading for their country,

In its hour of woe –

For the soldiers marching

Shoeless through the snow.

Lost in heavy slumbers,

Free from toil and strife,

Dreaming of their dear ones –

Home, and child, and wife –

Tentless they are lying,

While the fires burn low –

Lying in their blankets

'Midst December's snow.

MARGARET JUNKIN PRESTON

Only a Private

Only a private! his jacket of gray
Is stained by the smoke and the dust;
As Bayard he's brave, as Rupert he's gay,
Reckless as Murat in heat of the fray,
But in God is his only trust!

Only a private! to march and fight,
Suffer and starve and be strong;
With knowledge enough to know that the might
Of justice and truth, and freedom and right
In the end must crush out the wrong!

Only a private! no ribbon or star
Shall gild with false glory his name!
No honors for him in braid or in bar,
His Legion of Honor is only a scar,
And his wounds are his roll of fame!

Only a private! one more hero slain

On the field lies silent and chill!

And in the far South a wife prays in vain –

One clasp of the hands she may ne'er clasp again,

One kiss from the lips that are still!

Only a private! there let him sleep,

He will need no tablet nor stone;

For the mosses and vines o'er his grave will creep,

And at night the stars through the clouds will peep

And watch him who lies there alone!

Only a martyr! who fought and who fell,

Unknown and unmarked in the strife;

But still as he lies in his lonely cell,

Angel and seraph the legend shall tell –

Such a death is eternal life.

F. W. D.

Ashby

To the brave all homage render,
Weep, ye skies of June!
With a radiance pure and tender,
Shine, oh saddened moon!
"Dead upon the field of glory,"
Hero fit for song and story,
Lies our bold dragoon.

Well they learned, whose hands have slain him,
Braver, knightlier foe
Never fought with Moor nor Paynim,
Rode at Templestowe,
With a mien how high and joyous,
'Gainst the hordes that would destroy us
Went he forth we know.

Never more, alas! shall sabre
Gleam around his crest;
Fought his fight; fulfilled his labor;
Stilled his manly breast.

All unheard sweet Nature's cadence,

Trump of fame and voice of maidens,

Now he takes his rest.

Earth, that all too soon hath bound him,

Gently wrap his clay;

Linger lovingly around him,

Light of dying day;

Softly fall the summer showers;

Birds and bees among the flowers

Make the gloom seem gay.

There, throughout the coming ages,

When his sword is rust,

And his deeds in classic pages,

Mindful of her trust,

Shall Virginia, bending lowly,

Still a ceaseless vigil holy

Keep above his dust!

JOHN REUBEN THOMPSON

Stonewall Jackson's Way

Come, stack arms, men; pile on the rails;

Stir up the camp-fire bright!

No growling if the canteen fails;

We'll make a roaring night.

Here Shenandoah brawls along,

Here burly Blue Ridge echoes strong,

To swell the brigade's rousing song,

Of "Stonewall Jackson's way."

We see him now – the queer slouch hat

Cocked o'er his eye askew;

The shrewd, dry smile; the speech so pat,

So calm, so blunt, so true.

The "Bluelight Elder" knows 'em well;

Says he, "That's Banks; he's fond of shell.

Lord, save his soul! We'll give him" – well,

That's Stonewall Jackson's way.

Silence! Ground arms! Kneel all! Caps off!

Old Massa's going to pray.

Strangle the fool that dares to scoff.

Attention! it's his way.

Appealing from his native sod,

In forma pauperis to God,

"Lay bare thine arm! Stretch forth thy rod.

Amen." That's Stonewall's way.

He's in the saddle now. Fall in,

Steady the whole brigade!

Hill's at the ford, cut off; we'll win

His way out, ball and blade.

What matter if our shoes are worn?

What matter if our feet are torn?

Quick step! We're with him before morn –

That's Stonewall Jackson's way.

The sun's bright lances rout the mists

Of morning; and, by George!

Here's Longstreet, struggling in the lists,

Hemmed in an ugly gorge.

Pope and his Dutchmen! whipped before.

"Bay'nets and grape!" hear Stonewall roar.

Charge, Stuart! Pay off Ashby's score

In Stonewall Jackson's way.

Ah! maiden, wait and watch and yearn

For news of Stonewall's band.

Ah! widow, read with eyes that burn

That ring upon thy hand.

Ah! wife, sew on, pray on, hope on;

Thy life shall not be all forlorn;

The foe had better ne'er been born

That gets in Stonewall's way.

JOHN WILLIAMSON PALMER

Christmas Night of '62

The wintry blast goes wailing by,
The snow is falling overhead;
I hear the lonely sentry's tread,
And distant watch-fires light the sky.

Dim forms go flitting through the gloom;
The soldiers cluster round the blaze
To talk of other Christmas days,
And softly speak of home and home.

My sabre swinging overhead
Gleams in the watch-fire's fitful glow,
While fiercely drives the blinding snow,
And memory leads me to the dead.

My thoughts go wandering to and fro,
Vibrating 'twixt the Now and Then;
I see the low-browed home again,
The old hall wreathed with mistletoe.

And sweetly from the far-off years
Comes borne the laughter faint and low,
The voices of the Long Ago!
My eyes are wet with tender tears.

I feel again the mother-kiss,
I see again the glad surprise
That lightened up the tranquil eyes
And brimmed them o'er with tears of bliss,

As, rushing from the old hall-door,
She fondly clasped her wayward boy –
Her face all radiant with the joy
She felt to see him home once more.

My sabre swinging on the bough
Gleams in the watch-fire's fitful glow,
While fiercely drives the blinding snow
Aslant upon my saddened brow.

Those cherished faces all are gone!
Asleep within the quiet graves
Where lies the snow in drifting waves, –
And I am sitting here alone.

There's not a comrade here to-night
But knows that loved ones far away
On bended knees this night will pray:
"God bring our darling from the fight."

But there are none to wish me back,
For me no yearning prayers arise.
The lips are mute and closed the eyes –
My home is in the bivouac.

WILLIAM GORDON MCCABE

The Jacket of Gray

Fold it up carefully, lay it aside;

Tenderly touch it, look on it with pride;

For dear to our hearts must it be evermore,

The jacket of gray our loved soldier-boy wore.

Can we ever forget when he joined the brave band

That rose in defense of our dear Southern land,

And in his bright youth hurried on to the fray,

How proudly he donned it – the jacket of gray?

His fond mother blessed him, and looked up above,

Commending to heaven the child of her love;

What anguish was hers mortal tongue can not say,

When he passed from her sight in the jacket of gray.

But her country had called and she would not repine,

Though costly the sacrifice placed on its shrine;

Her heart's dearest hopes on its altar she lay,

When she sent out her boy in the jacket of gray.

Months passed, and war's thunder rolled over the land,

Unsheathed was the sword, and lighted the brand;

We heard in the distance the sound of the fray,

And prayed for our boy in the jacket of gray.

Ah vain, all in vain, were our prayers and our tears,

The glad shout of victory rang in our ears;

But our treasured one on the red battle-field lay,

While the life-blood oozed out on the jacket of gray.

His young comrades found him, and tenderly bore

The cold lifeless form to his home by the shore;

Oh, dark were our hearts on that terrible day,

When we saw our dead boy in the jacket of gray.

Ah! spotted and tattered, and stained now with gore,

Was the garment which once he so proudly wore;

We bitterly wept as we took it away,

And replaced with death's white robe the jacket of gray.

We laid him to rest in his cold narrow bed,

And graved on the marble we placed o'er his head

As the proudest tribute our sad hearts could pay –

"He never disgraced it, the jacket of gray."

Then fold it up carefully, lay it aside,

Tenderly touch it, look on it with pride;

For dear must it be to our hearts evermore,

The jacket of gray our loved soldier-boy wore!

CAROLINE A. BALL

Only One Killed

Only one killed – in company B
'Twas a trifling loss – one man!
A charge of the bold and dashing Lee –
While merry enough it was to see
The enemy, as he ran.

Only one killed upon our side –
Once more to the field they turn.
Quietly now the horsemen ride –
And pause by the form of the one who died
So bravely, as now we learn.

Their grief for the comrade loved and true
For a time was unconcealed;
They saw the bullet had pierced him through,
That his pain was brief – ah! very few
Die thus, on the battle-field.

The news has gone to his home, afar –
Of the short and gallant fight,
Of the noble deeds of the young La Var
Whose life went out as a falling star
In the skirmish of that night.

"Only one killed! It was my son,"
The widowed mother cried.
She turned but to clasp the sinking one,
Who heard not the words of the victory won,
But of him who had bravely died.

Ah! death to her were a sweet relief,
The bride of a single year.
Oh! would she might, with her weight of grief,
Lie down in the dust, with the autumn leaf
Now trodden and brown and sere!

But no, she must bear through coming life

Her burden of silent woe,

The aged mother and youthful wife

Must live through a nation's bloody strife,

Sighing and waiting to go.

Where the loved are meeting beyond the stars,

Are meeting no more to part.

They can smile once more through the crystal bars –

Where never more will the woe of wars

O'ershadow the loving heart.

JULIA L. KEYES

The Unknown Dead

The rain is plashing on my sill,

But all the winds of Heaven are still;

And so it falls with that dull sound

Which thrills us in the church-yard ground,

When the first spadeful drops like lead

Upon the coffin of the dead.

Beyond my streaming window-pane,

I cannot see the neighboring vane,

Yet from its old familiar tower

The bell comes, muffled, through the shower.

What strange and unsuspected link

Of feeling touched, has made me think –

While with a vacant soul and eye

I watch the gray and stony sky –

Of nameless graves on battle-plains

Washed by a single winter's rains,

Where, some beneath Virginian hills,

And some by green Atlantic rills,

Some by the waters of the West,

A myriad unknown heroes rest.

Ah! not the chiefs, who, dying, see

Their flags in front of victory,

Or, at their life-blood's noble cost
Pay for a battle nobly lost,
Claim from their monumental beds
The bitterest tears a nation sheds.
Beneath yon lonely mound – the spot
By all save some fond few forgot –
Lie the true martyrs of the fight
Which strikes for freedom and for right.
Of them, their patriot zeal and pride,
The lofty faith that with them died,
No grateful page shall farther tell
Than that so many bravely fell;
And we can only dimly guess
What worlds of all this world's distress,
What utter woe, despair, and dearth,
Their fate has brought to many a hearth.
Just such a sky as this should weep
Above them, always, where they sleep;
Yet, haply, at this very hour,
Their graves are like a lover's bower;
And Nature's self, with eyes unwet,
Oblivious of the crimson debt
To which she owes her April grace,
Laughs gayly o'er their burial-place.

HENRY TIMROD

The Dying Words of
Stonewall Jackson

"Order A.P. Hill to prepare for battle."

"Tell Major Hawks to advance the Commissary train."

"Let us cross the river and rest in the shade."

The stars of Night contain the glittering Day
And rain his glory down with sweeter grace
Upon the dark World's grand, enchanted face –
All loth to turn away.

And so the Day, about to yield his breath,
Utters the stars unto the listening Night,
To stand for burning fare-thee-wells of light
Said on the verge of death.

O hero-life that lit us like the sun!
O hero-words that glittered like the stars
And stood and shone above the gloomy wars
When the hero-life was done!

The phantoms of a battle came to dwell
I' the fitful vision of his dying eyes –
Yet even in battle-dreams, he sends supplies
To those he loved so well.

His army stands in battle-line arrayed:
His couriers fly: all's done: now God decide!
– And not till then saw he the Other Side
Or would accept the shade.

Thou Land whose sun is gone, thy stars remain!
Still shine the words that miniature his deeds.
O thrice-beloved, where'er thy great heart bleeds,
Solace hast thou for pain!

SIDNEY LANIER

Under the Shade of the Trees

What are the thoughts that are stirring his breast?
What is the mystical vision he sees?
– "Let us pass over the river, and rest
Under the shade of the trees."

Has he grown sick of his toils and his tasks?
Sighs the worn spirit for respite or ease?
Is it a moment's cool halt that he asks
"Under the shade of the trees."

Is it the gurgle of waters whose flow
Ofttime has come to him, borne on the breeze,
Memory listens to, lapsing so low,
Under the shade of the trees?

Nay – though the rasp of the flesh was so sore,
Faith, that had yearnings far keener than these,
Saw the soft sheen of the Thitherward Shore
Under the shade of the trees; –

Caught the high psalms of ecstatic delight –
Heard the harps harping, like soundings of seas –
Watched earth's assoiled ones walking in white
Under the shade of the trees.

Oh, was it strange he should pine for release,
Touched to the soul with such transports as these, –
He who so needed the balsam of peace,
Under the shade of the trees?

Yea, it was noblest for him – it was best
(Questioning naught of our Father's decrees),
There to pass over the river and rest
Under the shade of the trees!

MARGARET JUNKIN PRESTON

John Pelham

Just as the spring came laughing through the strife
With all its gorgeous cheer;
In the bright April of historic life
Fell the great cannoneer.

The wondrous lulling of a hero's breath
His bleeding country weeps –
Hushed in the alabaster arms of death,
Our young Marcellus sleeps.

Nobler and grander than the Child of Rome,
Curbing his chariot steeds;
The knightly scion of a Southern home
Dazzled the land with deeds.

Gentlest and bravest in the battle brunt,
The champion of the truth,
He bore his banner to the very front
Of our immortal youth.

A clang of sabres 'mid Virginian snow,

    The fiery pag of shells –

And there's a wail of immemorial woe

    In Alabama dells.

The pennon drops that led the sacred band

    Along the crimson field!

The meteor blade sinks from the nerveless hand

    Over the spotless shield.

We gazed and gazed upon that beauteous face,

    While 'round the lips and eyes,

Couched in the marble slumber, flashed the grace

    Of a divine surprise.

Oh, mother of a blessed soul on high!

    Thy tears may soon be shed –

Think of thy boy with princes of the sky,

    Among the Southern dead.

How must he smile on this dull world beneath,

    Fevered with swift renown –

He – with the martyr's amaranthine wreath

    Twining the victor's crown!

JAMES RYDER RANDALL

Ode

Sleep sweetly in your humble graves,
  Sleep, martyrs of a fallen cause;
Though yet no marble column craves
  The pilgrim here to pause.

In seeds of laurel in the earth,
  The blossom of your fame is blown,
And somewhere, waiting for its birth,
  The shaft is in the stone.

Meanwhile, behalf the tardy years
  Which keep in trust your storied tombs,
Behold your sisters bring their tears,
  And these memorial blooms.

Small tributes but your shades will smile
More proudly on these wreaths today,
Than when some cannon-moulded pile
Shall overlook this bay.

Stoop, angels, hither from the skies,
There is no holier spot of ground,
Than where defeated valor lies,
By mourning beauty crowned.

HENRY TIMROD

Lee to the Rear

(May 6, 1864)

Dawn of a pleasant morning in May
Broke through the Wilderness cool and gray;
While perched in the tallest tree-top, the birds
Were carolling Mendelssohn's "Songs without Words."

Far from the haunts of men remote,
The brook brawled on with a liquid note;
And Nature, all tranquil and lovely, wore
The smile of the spring, as in Eden of yore.

Little by little, as daylight increased,
And deepened the roseate flush in the East –
Little by little did morning reveal
Two long glittering lines of steel;

Where two hundred thousand bayonets gleam,
Tipped with the light of the earliest beam,
And the faces are sullen and grim to see
In the hostile armies of Grant and Lee.

All of a sudden, ere rose the sun,

Pealed on the silence the opening gun –

A little white puff of smoke there came,

And anon the valley was wreathed in flame.

Down on the left of the Rebel lines,

Where a breastwork stands in a copse of pines,

Before the Rebels their ranks can form,

The Yankees have carried the place by storm.

Stars and Stripes on the salient wave,

Where many a hero has found a grave,

And the gallant Confederates strive in vain

The ground they have drenched with their blood, to regain.

Yet louder the thunder of battle roared –

Yet a deadlier fire on the columns poured;

Slaughter infernal rode with Despair,

Furies twain, through the murky air.

Not far off, in the saddle there sat
A gray-bearded man in a black slouched hat;
Not much moved by the fire was he,
Calm and resolute Robert Lee.

Quick and watchful he kept his eye
On the bold Rebel brigades close by, –
Reserves that were standing (and dying) at ease,
While the tempest of wrath toppled over the trees.

For still with their loud, deep, bull-dog bay,
The Yankee batteries blazed away,
And with every murderous second that sped
A dozen brave fellows, alas! fell dead.

The grand old graybeard rode to the space
Where Death and his victims stood face to face,
And silently waved his old slouched hat –
A world of meaning there was in that!

"Follow me! Steady! We'll save the day!"

This was what he seemed to say;

And to the light of his glorious eye

The bold brigades thus made reply:

"We'll go forward, but you must go back" –

And they moved not an inch in the perilous track:

"Go to the rear, and we'll send them to hell!"

And the sound of the battle was lost in their yell.

Turning his bridle, Robert Lee

Rode to the rear. Like waves of the sea,

Bursting the dikes in their overflow,

Madly his veterans dashed on the foe.

And backward in terror that foe was driven,

Their banners rent and their columns riven

Wherever the tide of battle rolled

Over the Wilderness, wood and wold.

Sunset out of a crimson sky
Streamed o'er a field of ruddier dye,
And the brook ran on with a purple stain,
From the blood of ten thousand foemen slain.

Seasons have passed since that day and year –
Again o'er its pebbles the brook runs clear,
And the field in a richer green is drest
Where the dead of a terrible conflict rest.

Hushed is the roll of the Rebel drum,
The sabres are sheathed, and the cannon are dumb;
And Fate, with his pitiless hand, has furled
The flag that once challenged the gaze of the world;

But the fame of the Wilderness fight abides;
And down into history grandly rides,
Calm and unmoved as in battle he sat,
The gray-bearded man in the black slouched hat.

JOHN REUBEN THOMPSON

The Two Armies

Two armies stand enrolled beneath
The banner with the starry wreath;
One, facing battle, blight and blast,
Through twice a hundred fields has passed;
Its deeds against a ruffian foe,
Stream, valley, hill, and mountain know,
Till every wind that sweeps the land
Goes, glory-laden, from the strand.

The other, with a narrower scope,
Yet led by not less grand a hope,
Hath won, perhaps, as proud a place,
And wears its fame with meeker grace.
Wives march beneath its glittering sign,
Fond mothers swell the lovely line;
And many a sweetheart hides her blush
In the young patriot's generous flush.

No breeze of battle ever fanned
The colors of that tender band;
Its office is beside the bed,

Where throbs some sick or wounded head.
It does not court the soldier's tomb,
But plies the needle and the loom;
And, by a thousand peaceful deeds,
Supplies a struggling nation's needs.

Nor is that army's gentle night
Unfelt amid the deadly fight;
It nerves the son's, the husband's hand,
It points the lover's fearless brand;
It thrills the languid, warms the cold,
Gives even new courage to the bold.
And sometimes lifts the veriest clod
To its own lofty trust in God.

When Heaven shall blow the trump of peace,
And bid this weary warfare cease,
Their several missions nobly done,
The triumph grasped, and freedom won,
Both armies, from their toils at rest,
Alike may claim the victor's crest,
But each shall see its dearest prize
Gleam softly from the other's eyes.

HENRY TIMROD

Cleburne

Another ray of light hath fled, another Southern brave
Hath fallen in his country's cause and found a laureled grave –
Hath fallen, but his deathless name shall live when stars shall set,
For, noble Cleburne, thou art one this world will ne'er forget.

'Tis true, thy warm heart beats no more, that on thy noble head
Azrael placed his icy hand, and thou art with the dead;
The glancing of thine eyes are dim; no more will they be bright
Until they ope in Paradise, with clearer, heavenlier light.

No battle news disturbs thy rest upon the sun-bright shore,
No clarion voice awakens thee on earth to wrestle more,
No tramping steed, no wary foe bids thee awake, arise,
For thou art in the angel world, beyond the starry skies.

Brave Cleburne, dream in thy low bed, with pulseless
deadened heart;
Calm, calm and sweet, O warrior rest! thou well hast
borne thy part,

And now a glory wreath for thee the angels singing twine,
A glory wreath, not of the earth, but made by hands divine.

A long farewell – we give thee up, with all thy bright renown,
A chieftain here on earth is lost, in heaven an angel found.
Above thy grave a wail is heard – a nation mourns her dead;
A nobler for the South ne'er died, a braver never bled.

A last farewell – how can we speak the bitter word farewell!
The anguish of our bleeding hearts vain words may never tell.
Sleep on, sleep on, to God we give our chieftain in his might;
And weeping, feel he lives on high, where comes no sorrow's night.

AUTHOR UNKNOWN

Dreaming in the Trenches

I picture her there in the quaint old room,
Where the fading fire-light starts and falls,
Alone in the twilight's tender gloom
With the shadows that dance on the dim-lit walls.

Alone, while those faces look silently down
From their antique frames in a grim repose —
Slight scholarly Ralph in his Oxford gown,
And stanch Sir Alan, who died for Montrose.

There are gallants gay in crimson and gold,
There are smiling beauties with powdered hair,
But she sits there, fairer a thousand-fold,
Leaning dreamily back in her low arm-chair.

And the roseate shadows of fading light
Softly clear steal over the sweet young face,
Where a woman's tenderness blends to-night
With the guileless pride of a knightly race.

Her hands lie clasped in a listless way
On the old *Romance* – which she holds on her knee –
Of *Tristram*, the bravest of knights in the fray,
And Iseult, who waits by the sounding sea.

And her proud, dark eyes wear a softened look
As she watches the dying embers fall:
Perhaps she dreams of the knight in the book,
Perhaps of the pictures that smile on the wall.

What fancies I wonder are thronging her brain,
For her cheeks flush warm with a crimson glow!
Perhaps – ah! me, how foolish and vain!
But I'd give my life to believe it so!

Well, whether I ever march home again
To offer my love and a stainless name,
Or whether I die at the head of my men, –
I'll be true to the end all the same.

WILLIAM GORDON MCCABE

Your Letter, Lady, Came Too Late

Your letter, lady, came too late,
For Heaven had claimed its own.
Ah, sudden change – from prison rats
Unto the great white throne!
And yet I think he would have stayed
To live for his disdain,
Could he have read the careless words
Which you have sent in vain.

So full of patience did he wait
Through many a weary hour,
That o'er his simple soldier faith
Not even death had power.
And you – did others whisper low
Their homage in your ear,
As though among their shadowy throng
His spirit had a peer.

I would that you were by me now,
To draw the sheet aside,
And see how pure the look he wore

The moment when he died.
The sorrow that you gave him
Had left its weary trace,
As 'twere the shadow of the cross
Upon his pallid face.

"Her love," he said, "could change for me
The winter's cold to spring."
Ah, trust of fickle maiden's love,
Thou art a bitter thing!
For when these valleys bright in May
Once more with blossoms wave,
The northern violets shall blow
Above his humble grave.

Your dole of scanty words had been
But one more pang to bear,
For him who kissed unto the last
Your tress of golden hair.
I did not put it where he said,
For when the angels come
I would not have them find the sign
Of falsehood in the tomb.

I've seen your letter and I know
The wiles that you have wrought
To win that noble heart of his,
And gained it – cruel thought!
What lavish wealth men sometimes give
For what is worthless all:
What manly bosoms beat for them
In folly's falsest thrall.

You shall not pity him, for now
His sorrow has an end,
Yet would that you could stand with me
Beside my fallen friend.
And I forgive you for his sake
As he – if it be given –
May even be pleading grace for you
Before the court of Heaven.

Tonight the cold wind whistles by
As I, my vigil keep
Within the prison dead house, where
Few mourners come to weep.

A rude plank coffin holds his form,

Yet death exalts his face

And I would rather see him thus

Than clasped in your embrace.

Tonight your home may shine with lights

And ring with merry song,

And you be smiling as your soul

Had done no deadly wrong.

Your hand so fair that none would think

It penned these words of pain;

Your skin so white – would God, your heart

Were half as free from stain.

I'd rather be my comrade dead,

Than you in life supreme:

For yours the sinner's waking dread,

And his the martyr's dream.

Whom serve we in this life we serve

In that which is to come:

He chose his way, you yours; let God

Pronounce the fitting doom.

W.S. HAWKINS

John Pegram

What shall we say, now, of our gentle knight,
Or how express the measure of our woe,
For him who rode the foremost in the fight,
Whose good blade flashed so far amid the foe?

Of all his knightly deeds what need to tell? –
That good blade now lies fast within its sheath;
What can we do but point to where he fell,
And, like a soldier, met a soldier's death?

We sorrow not as those who have no hope;
For he was pure in heart as brave in deed –
God pardon us, if blindly we should grope,
And love be questioned by the hearts that bleed.

And yet – oh! foolish and of little faith!
We cannot choose but weep our useless tears;
We loved him so; we never dreamed that death
Would dare to touch him in his brave young years.

Ah, dear, browned face, so fearless and so bright!
    As kind to friend as thou wast stern to foe –
    No more we'll see thee radiant in the fight,
    The eager eyes – the flush on cheek and brow!

    No more we'll greet the lithe, familiar form,
    Amid the surging smoke, with deaf'ning cheer;
    No more shall soar above the iron storm,
    Thy ringing voice in accents sweet and clear.

    Aye! he has fought the fight and passed away –
    Our grand young leader smitten in the strife!
    So swift to seize the chances of the fray,
    And careless only of his noble life.

    He is not dead but sleepeth! well we know
    The form that lies to-day beneath the sod,
    Shall rise that time the golden bugles blow,
    And pour their music through the courts of God.

And there amid our great heroic dead –

The war-worn sons of God, whose work is done –

His face shall shine, as they with stately tread,

In grand review, sweep past the jasper throne.

Let not our hearts be troubled, few and brief

His days were here, yet rich in love and faith;

Lord, we believe, help thou our unbelief,

And grant thy servants such a life and death!

WILLIAM GORDON MCCABE

Little Giffen

Out of the focal and foremost fire,

Out of the hospital walls as dire,

Smitten of grape-shot and gangrene

(Eighteenth battle and he sixteen) –

Spectre such as you seldom see,

Little Giffen of Tennessee.

"Take him – and welcome!" the surgeons said,

"Little the doctor can help the dead!"

So we took him and brought him where

The balm was sweet on the summer air;

And we laid him down on a wholesome bed –

Utter Lazarus, heel to head!

And we watched the war with bated breath –

Skeleton Boy against skeleton Death.

Months of torture, how many such!

Weary weeks of the stick and crutch;

And still a glint in the steel-blue eye

Told of a spirit that wouldn't die.

And didn't. Nay, more! in death's despite
The crippled skeleton learned to write.
"Dear Mother," at first, of course; and then
"Dear Captain," inquiring about "the men."
Captain's answer: "Of eighty and five,
Giffen and I are left alive."

Word of gloom from the war one day:
"Johnston's pressed at the front, they say!"
Little Giffen was up and away;
A tear – his first – as he bade good-by,
Dimmed the glint of his steel-blue eye.
"I'll write, if spared!" There was news of the fight:
But none of Giffen – he did not write.

I sometimes fancy that, were I king
Of the princely knights of the Golden Ring,
With the song of the minstrel in mine ear,
And the tender legend that trembles here,
I'd give the best, on his bended knee,
The whitest soul of my chivalry,
For Little Giffen of Tennessee.

FRANCIS ORRAY TICKNOR

C.S.A.

Do we weep for the heroes who died for us,
Who living were true and tried for us,
And dying sleep side by side for us;
The Martyr-band
That hallowed our land
With the blood they shed in a tide for us?

Ah! fearless on many a day for us
They stood in front of the fray for us,
And held the foeman at bay for us;
And tears should fall
Fore'er o'er all
Who fell while wearing the Gray for us.

How many a glorious name for us,
How many a story of fame for us
They left: Would it not be a blame for us
If their memories part
From our land and heart,
And a wrong to them, and shame for us?

No, no, no, they were brave for us,

And bright were the lives they gave for us;

The land they struggled to save for us

Will not forget

Its warriors yet

Who sleep in so many a grave for us.

On many and many a plain for us

Their blood poured down all in vain for us,

Red, rich, and pure, like a rain for us;

They bleed – we weep,

We live – they sleep,

"All lost," the only refrain for us.

But their memories e'er shall remain for us,

And their names, bright names, without stain for us;

The glory they won shall not wane for us,

In legend and lay

Our heroes in Gray

Shall forever live over again for us.

ABRAM JOSEPH RYAN

Acceptation

We do accept thee, heavenly Peace!
Albeit thou comest in a guise
Unlooked for – undesired, our eyes
Welcome through tears the sweet release
From war, and woe, and want, – surcease,
For which we bless thee, blessed Peace!

We lift our foreheads from the dust;
And as we meet thy brow's clear calm,
There falls a freshening sense of balm
Upon our spirits. Fear – distrust –
The hopeless present on us thrust –
We'll meet them as we can, and *must*.

War has not wholly wrecked us; still
Strong hands, brave hearts, high souls are ours –
Proud consciousness of quenchless powers –
A Past whose memory makes us thrill –
Futures uncharactered, to fill
With heroisms – if we will.

Then courage, brothers! – Though each breast

Feel oft the rankling thorn, despair,

That failure plants so sharply there –

No pain, no pang shall be confest:

We'll work and watch the brightening west,

And leave to God and Heaven, the rest.

MARGARET JUNKIN PRESTON

Lines on the Back of a Confederate Note

Representing nothing on God's earth now,
And naught in the water below it –
As pledge of the nation that's dead and gone,
Keep it, dear friend, and show it.

Show it to those who will lend an ear
To the tale that this paper can tell
Of liberty born, of patriot's dream –
Of the storm cradled nation that fell.

Too poor to possess the precious ores,
And too much of a stranger to borrow,
We issued today our promise to pay,
And hope to redeem on the morrow.

The days rolled on and weeks became years,
But our coffers were empty still,
Coin was so rare that the Treasury quaked,
If a dollar should drop in the till.

But the faith that was in us was strong indeed,
And our poverty well discerned;
And these little checks represented the pay,
That our volunteers earned.

We know it had hardly value in gold,
Yet as gold her soldier received it.
It gazed in our eyes with a promise to pay,
And each patriot soldier believed it.

But our boys thought little of price of pay,
Or of bills that were ever due;
We knew if it brought us bread today,
'Twas the best our poor country could do.

Keep it, for it tells our history o'er,
From the birth of its dreams to the last,
Modest and born of the angel Hope,
Like the hope of success it passed.

S.A. JONAS

The Conquered Banner

Furl that Banner, for 'tis weary;
Round its staff 'tis drooping dreary;
Furl it, fold it, it is best;
For there's not a man to wave it,
And there's not a sword to save it,
And there's not one left to lave it
In the blood which heroes gave it;
And its foes now scorn and brave it;
Furl it, hide it – let it rest!

Take that banner down! 'tis tattered;
Broken is its staff and shattered;
And the valiant hosts are scattered
Over whom it floated high.
Oh! 'tis hard for us to fold it;
Hard to think there's none to hold it;
Hard that those who once unrolled it
Now must furl it with a sigh.

Furl that Banner! furl it sadly!
Once ten thousands hailed it gladly,
And ten thousands wildly, madly,
Swore it should forever wave;
Swore that foeman's sword should never
Hearts like theirs entwined dissever,
Till that flag should float forever
O'er their freedom or their grave!

Furl it; for the hands that grasped it,
And the hearts that fondly clasped it,
Cold and dead are lying low;
And that Banner – it is trailing!
While around it sounds the wailing
Of its people in their woe.

For, though conquered, they adore it!
Love the cold, dead hands that bore it!
Weep for those who fell before it!
Pardon those who trailed and tore it!

But, oh! wildly they deplore it,
Now who furl and fold it so.

Furl that Banner! True, 'tis gory,
Yet 'tis wreathed around with glory,
And 'twill live in song and story,
Though its folds are in the dust:
For its fame on brightest pages,
Penned by poets and by sages,
Shall go sounding down the ages –
Furl its folds though now we must.

Furl that Banner, softly, slowly!
Treat it gently – it is holy –
For it droops above the dead.
Touch it not – unfold it never,
Let it droop there, furled forever,
For its people's hopes are dead!

ABRAM JOSEPH RYAN

Ashes of Glory

Fold up the gorgeous silken sun,
By blending martyrs blest,
And heap the laurels it has won
Above its place of rest.

No trumpet's note need harshly blare –
No drum funereal roll –
No trailing sables drape the bier
That frees a dauntless soul.

It lived with Lee, and decked his brow
From fate's empyreal Palm
It sleeps the sleep of Jackson now –
As spotless and as calm.

It was outnumbered – not outdone;
And they shall shuddering tell
Who struck the blow, its latest gun
Flashed ruin as it fell.

Sleep, shrouded ensign! Not the breeze
That smote the victor tar
With death across the heaving seas
Of fiery Trafalgar;

Not Arthur's Knights amid the gloom
Their knightly deeds have starred;
Nor Gallic Henry's matchless plume,
Nor peerless-born Bayard.

Not all that antique fables feign,
And orient dreams disgorge;
Not yet the silver cross of Spain,
And Lion of St. George,

Can bid thee pale! Proud emblem, still
Thy crimson glory shines
Beyond the lengthened shades that fill
Their proudest kingly lines.

Sleep! in thine own historic night –
And be thy blazoned scroll;
A warrior's banner takes its flight
To greet the warrior's soul.

AUGUSTUS JULIAN REQUIER

BIOGRAPHIES

CAROLINE A. BALL (NÉE RUTLEDGE) was born in Charleston, South Carolina, in 1825. A slim volume of her verse, *The Jacket of Gray, and Other Fugitive Poems*, was published in 1866.

ETHEL LYNN BEERS (1827–1879) was born Ethelinda Eliot in Goshen, New York. She began writing at an early age, her work appearing under the name Ethel Lynn, until her marriage, in 1846, to William H. Beers. Her best-known poem, 'All Quiet Along the Potomac', first appeared as 'The Picket Guard' in the November 30, 1861 issue of *Harper's Weekly Magazine*. One of the most popular of the war, the poem was reprinted often and frequently claimed by others. Beers was the author of two books, *General Frankie: A Story for Little Folks (1863)* and *All Quiet Along the Potomac and Other Poems (1879)*, the latter published the day before she died.

AMBROSE BIERCE (1842–1914?) was born into a farming family near Horse Cave Creek, Ohio. During the war he served in the Union Army's Ninth Indiana Infantry. In June 1864, Bierce's wartime service ended after he received a head wound at the Battle of Kennesaw Mountain. Following the war, he embarked on a number of careers, the longest and most successful of which was as a newspaperman for William Randolph Hearst. In 1913, Bierce headed south, intending to report on the Mexican Revolution. He served as an observer in Pancho Villa's army, and was last heard from on December 26, 1913. His disappearance remains one of the great mysteries in American literature. Bierce was the author of many books, the most popular being *The Devil's Dictionary*, originally published in 1906 as *The Cynic's Word Book*.

GEORGE HENRY BOKER (1823–1890), the son of a wealthy Philadelphia banker, was educated at the College of New Jersey (now Princeton University). His first book of verse, *The Lessons of Life, and Other Poems*, was published in 1848, as was the play *Calaynos* which launched Boker's career as a playwright. During the Civil War he turned his talents to the writing of patriotic verse. Boker was also the founder of the Union League Club, an organization dedicated to raising funds for the war effort. His involvement with politics continued after the war as US Minister to Turkey and Russia.

CAROLINE, the author of 'Farewell to Brother Jonathan', remains unknown. The poem, a response to 'Brother Jonathan's Lament for Sister Caroline' by Oliver Wendell Holmes Sr, dates back to at least 1864.

JANET T.H. CROSS was an educator who operated a school in Nashville. She was a prolific writer of Confederate poetry and was the author of at least two works of fiction, the Civil War novella *David Adair* (1864) and *Azile* (1868).

F.W.D was the pen name of **FRANCIS WARRINGTON DAWSON** (1840–1889). Born Austin John Reeks in London, England, Dawson served in both the Confederate Army and Navy. He recorded his wartime experiences in *Reminiscences of Confederate Service*, 1861–1865 (1882). After the war, Dawson became editor of *The News and Courier* in Charleston. Dawson was twice married, the second time to journalist and memoirist Sarah Morgan, author of *A Confederate Girl's Diary* (1913).

EMILY DICKINSON (1830-1886) was born in Amherst, Massachusetts, to a prominent New England family. Though one of the great American poets, she saw only seven of her 1775 poems published, all of them anonymously. It wasn't until, *Poems*, the first collection of Dickinson's poetry, published four years after the poet's death, that her work began to receive proper notice.

RALPH WALDO EMERSON (1803-1882) was born in Boston, Massachusetts, the son of a Unitarian minister. He attended Harvard and, after graduation, worked as a teacher and schoolmaster. Emerson later attended Harvard Divinity School and, in 1829, became a Unitaritan minister. He resigned three years later, following a dispute with church officials. A leading thinker and essayist, much of Emerson's livelihood was derived from his skill as a public orator. His books often grew out of his lectures. Three collections of poetry, *Poems* (1847), *May-Day and Other Pieces* (1867), and *Selected Poems* (1876), were published during his lifetime.

FRANCIS MILES FINCH (1827-1907) was born in Ithaca, New York. A Yale graduate, he practiced law, served on the bench, and lectured at Cornell University, an institution he had helped to establish. A collection of his poetry, *The Blue and The Gray, and Other Verses* (1909) was published posthumously.

BRET HARTE (1836–1902) was born in Albany, New York. In 1854, he moved to California. He became a popular chronicler of California pioneer life through poems, stories, and sketches published in *The Californian and The Overland Monthly*, which he also edited. In 1878, he became a United States Consul and was appointed to Krefeld, Germany and, later, Glasgow. He eventually settled in London.

W. S. HAWKINS (1837–1865) was born in Madison County, Alabama. A student at the outbreak of the war, he enlisted and quickly rose to the rank of Colonel. In January 1864, Hawkins was captured and taken to Camp Chase in Ohio. Hawkins was released at the end of the war and died several months later.

OLIVER WENDELL HOLMES SR (1809–1894) was born in Cambridge, Massachusetts, and educated in Andover, Boston, and Paris. Although a prominent physician and professor of anatomy, he achieved greater fame as a poet of national prominence. His son, Supreme Court Justice Oliver Wendell Holmes Jr, served in the 20th Massachusetts Volunteer Infantry.

JULIA WARD HOWE (1819–1910) was born in New York City. At 23, she married physician Samuel Gridley Howe, a fellow abolitionist and educator. A prolific travel writer, playwright, and poet, Howe is best remembered for her anthem 'The Battle Hymn of the Republic'. The song, first published on the front page of an 1862 edition of *The Atlantic Monthly*, was one of the most popular of the war. She is also credited with the creation of Mother's Day, through her 1870 Mother's Day Proclamation. In later years, Howe became increasingly active in the Suffragette movement; particularly after the death of her husband.

S. A. JONAS (?–1915), a Confederate Major from Aberdeen, Mississippi. Following the conflict, he became founder and editor of *The Aberdeen Examiner*. Jonas claimed to have penned 'The Confederate Note' for New York actress Annie Rush on the back of a $500 CSA banknote shortly after the war's end. Although the poem, also known as 'The Lost Cause' and 'The Confederate Note', has been attributed to others, Abram Joseph Ryan among them, evidence points to Jonas as the author.

JULIA L. KEYES (1829–1877) was a little-known poet from Montgomery, Alabama. She is said to have written 'Only One Killed' after having read the phrase in a newspaper account of an 1864 battle. Following the war, she and her physician husband emigrated to Brazil.

SIDNEY LANIER (1842–1881) was born in Macon, Georgia. He enlisted in the Confederate Army and served in Virginia, North Carolina, and Florida. In 1863, he was captured and imprisoned, an experience which served to inspire a novel, *Tiger-Lilies* (1867). Lanier practiced law for a few years after the war, before settling into a career delivering lectures on English literature. A prolific writer, he was the author of a number of books, the bulk of which deal with literary scholarship. A collection of his verse, *Poems of Sidney Lanier* (1884), was published posthumously.

HENRY WADSWORTH LONGFELLOW (1807–1882) was born in Portland, Maine. He was educated at Bowdoin College in Brunswick, where he became a professor. After later accepting an appointment at Harvard, he relocated to Cambridge, Massachusetts, and lived there the rest of his life in a house that had been occupied by George Washington during the American Revolution. Longfellow was the most famous and well-loved American poet of his day. Among his more popular works are *Evangeline: A Tale of Acadie* (1847) and *The Song of Hiawatha* (1855). An ardent abolitionist, Longfellow's writing on the war, indeed the remainder of his life, was overshadowed by the horrific death of his second wife, from burns suffered in a fire, during the second month of the conflict.

WILLIAM GORDON MCCABE (1841–1920) was born in Richmond, Virginia. Following the state's withdrawal from the Union, he left his studies to enlist in the Confederate Army. A private in the Army of Northern Virginia, he soon rose to the rank of Captain. At the end of the hostilities, he returned to Virginia. He was the author of several books and edited several anthologies, including *Ballads of Battle and Bravery* (1873).

ALEXANDER B. MEEK (1814–1865) was born in Columbia, South Carolina. As a young man, he participated in the Second Seminole War. At the close of the campaign, he was appointed Attorney General of Alabama, the first of several public positions. Although a prolific writer, most of Meek's books, including *Songs and Poems of the South* (1857) and *Romantic Passages in Southwestern History* (1857), were composed during his final decade.

HERMAN MELVILLE (1819–1891) was born in New York City. His education was disrupted several times by bankruptcy and the death of his father. After finally leaving school, Melville found employment as a sailor and as a schoolteacher. His experiences as the former served to inspire the majority of his novels, including *Typee* (1846), *Omoo* (1847), and *Mardi* (1849). Melville's early work was quite popular, but his audience quickly declined. *Moby-Dick* (1851), his masterpiece, considered by many to be 'The Great American Novel', was a commercial failure. Melville's first collection of poetry, *Battle-Pieces and Aspects of the War: Civil War Poems* (1866), sold fewer than 500 copies. In middle age, he turned to public speaking and, for nearly two decades, worked as a customs inspector for the City of New York.

PRIVATE MILES O'REILLY was just one of many pen-names employed by **CHARLES GRAHAM HALPINE** (1829–1868). Born in County Meath, Ireland, Halpine studied medicine and law before settling into a career in journalism, contributing to a number of magazines and newspapers including *The New York Herald* and *The New York Times*. He then left journalism for a career in city politics. Shortly after the beginning of the war, on April 20, 1861, Halpine became a lieutenant in the 69th New York State Militia (later the 69th New York Volunteer Infantry). His poem 'The Thousand and Thirty-Seven', also known as 'April 20, 1864', is a celebration of the regiment. A successful officer, who rose to the rank of Brigadier General, failing eyesight forced Halpine's resignation in the summer of 1864. That same year saw publication of *Miles O'Reilly: His Book*, the first of two O'Reilly books. Halpine returned New York and resumed his work in journalism and city politics. He died in 1868.

JOHN WILLIAMSON PALMER (1825–1906) was born in Baltimore and studied medicine at the University of Maryland. He practiced in San Francisco and Honolulu, before being hired as a surgeon of the East India Company. From 1851 to 1852 Palmer served in the Second Burmese War, returning to the United States in 1853. During the Civil War, he enlisted in the Confederate Army and was a war correspondent for *The New York Tribune*. A poet, novelist, anthologist, and translator, Palmer was the author of numerous books, including *For Charlie's Sake and Other Lyrics and Ballads* (1901).

MARGARET JUNKIN PRESTON (1820-1897) was born in Philadelphia. Her sister, Elinore Junkin Jackson, was the first wife of Thomas Jonathan 'Stonewall' Jackson. Though Elinore died during childbirth some fourteen months into the marriage, Preston remained close to Jackson. There is some speculation that societal pressures prohibited a marriage. When war broke out, she sided with the Confederacy, much to the displeasure of her father, the Rev. Dr George Junkin, president of Washington College, a staunch Unionist. Preston was a popular poet in her day and published a number of collections of verse, the most notable being *Beechenbrook: A Rhyme of the War* (1865), in which 'Under the Shade of the Tree' is found.

JAMES RYDER RANDALL (1839-1908) was born in Baltimore. Ill health prevented him from serving in the conflict, but he wrote much in support of the Confederacy. After the war Randall settled in Augusta, Georgia, where he became editor-in-chief of *The Constitutionalist*.

THOMAS BUCHANAN READ (1822-1872) was born in Chester County, Pennsylvania. He ran away from home at an early age, supporting himself as a cigar maker, sign painter, and portrait artist. In 1843, his first poems were published in a Boston newspaper. His first collection of verse, *Poems*, was published four years later. Several other volumes followed, including *Summer Story, Sheridan's Ride, and Other Poems* (1865), which focused chiefly on the Civil War. Having settled in Europe, Read returned to the United States during the conflict. Read returned to Europe at the war's end.

AUGUSTUS JULIAN REQUIER (1825-1887) was born in Charleston, South Carolina. He began writing at an early age; his first book, *The Spanish Exile* (1842), a play in blank verse, was published at the age of seventeen. Two years later, he was admitted to the bar. In 1853, Requier was appointed United States district attorney, and held the equivalent position under the Confederate government. After the war, he decided to relocate to New York City where he became active in municipal politics.

JAMES JEFFREY ROCHE (1847-1908) was born in Queen's County, Ireland. He was raised and educated in Prince Edward Island, then a British colony. He emigrated to Boston in 1866, where he found editorial work on *The Pilot*. His first book, *Songs and Satires* was published in 1887.

ABRAM JOSEPH RYAN (1839–1886) was born in Norfolk, Virginia. The son of Irish immigrants, he became a Roman Catholic priest and served in the war as a chaplain in the Confederate Army. After the conflict, Ryan moved to New Orleans, where he edited *The Star*, a weekly Roman Catholic newspaper. He later relocated to Augusta, Georgia, where he founded a religious and political weekly, *The Banner of the South*. Ryan's writings were published in several volumes, the most popular being *Poems: Patriotic, Religious, and Miscellaneous* (1880).

CHARLES DAWSON SHANLY (1811–1875) was born and educated in Dublin, Ireland. As a young man, he emigrated to Canada, and held a position there in the civil service. His brother, Walter, was a confidant of the first Canadian Prime Minister, Sir John A. Macdonald. By 1860, Shanly had moved to New York, where he found work as a contributor of essays, poetry, and sketches to a variety of popular magazines and newspapers.

KATE BROWNLEE SHERWOOD (1841–1914) was born Katherine Brownlee in Poland, Ohio. She married during the war Isaac R. Sherwood, an officer in the Union Army, and future United States congressman. A frequent contributor to various newspapers and magazines, she was known as 'the poetess of the congressional circle'.

JOHN REUBEN THOMPSON (1823–1873) was born in Richmond, Virginia. He studied law at the University of Virginia. In 1847, he became the editor *The Southern Literary Messenger*. Thompson went on to edit several other Southern periodicals before emigrating to England during the war. After the conflict, he returned to the United States, settling in New York, where he became literary editor of *The New York Evening Post*.

FRANCIS ORRAY TICKNOR (1822–1874) was born in Fortville, Georgia. Having earned a medical degree from the Philadelphia College of Medicine in 1842, he set up a practice as a country doctor in Columbus, Georgia. Two collections of his poetry, *The Poems of Frank O. Ticknor, M. D.* (1879) and *The Poems of Francis Orray Ticknor* (1911), were published posthumously.

HENRY TIMROD (1829–1867) was born in Charleston, South Carolina, the son of a bookbinder and minor poet. The younger Timrod's first collection of verse, *Poems*, was published in 1860. An impassioned supporter of the Confederacy, he twice enlisted, but was discharged both times due to ill health. For a time he worked as a war correspondent for *The Charleston Mercury*. In 1864, he moved to Columbia, where he edited *The Daily South Carolinian*. When the city was burned in February 1865, Timrod was reduced to extreme poverty, from which he never recovered. His health continued to deteriorate and he died of tuberculosis.

CATHERINE M. WARFIELD (1816–1877) was born Catherine Ann Ware in Natchez, Mississippi. She was educated with her sister Eleanor in Philadelphia, and after marriage settled in Kentucky. Her first books, *The Wife of Leon and Other Poems* (1844) and *The Indian Chamber and Other Poems* (1846) were written with Eleanor. She later concentrated on fiction, writing 10 romances during the last 17 years of her life.

WALT WHITMAN (1819–1892) was born in West Hills, New York. After leaving school, he undertook a number of occupations, including printer, carpenter, teacher, and newspaper editor. Whitman's most important work, *Leaves of Grass*, was first published in 1855 as a slim volume containing 12 long poems. Whitman spent much of the rest of his life revising the work, adding and, occasionally, removing verse. The last edition, published the year before his death, contained nearly 400 poems. In 1862, after his brother, George Washington Whitman, was wounded in Fredericksburg, Virginia, Whitman volunteered as an army nurse and ministered to soldiers in Washington. He recorded his war-time experiences in *Drum-Taps* (1865) and *Memoranda During the* War (1867).

JOHN GREENLEAF WHITTIER (1807–1892) was born in Haverhill, Massachusetts. He received little in the way of formal education, yet made his literary debut at the age of 19. Whittier's first book, *Legends of New England*, was published in 1831. A dedicated abolitionist he entered politics and promoted the cause through his editorship of a number of influential periodicals. Whittier turned from politics after the Civil War and dedicated himself completely to poetry. His fame increased greatly with the publication of *Snow-Bound* (1866), a long narrative poem. In his time, Whittier was considered one of the great American poets, second only to Henry Wadsworth Longfellow. After his death several states declared holidays on his birthday.

INDEX OF POETS

INDEX OF TITLES

THE BLUE

THE GRAY

INDEX OF FIRST LINES

THE BLUE

THE GRAY